Maternity
Real stories of
motherhood

Francesca Newby

To Tom, Will and Sophie,
and Kiff, who helped me make them.

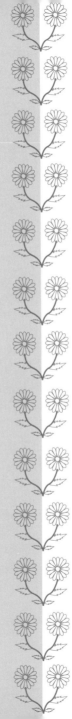

Real stories of motherhood

Maternity

Francesca Newby

Contents

'PERItHAPS WE SHARE STORIES IN MUCH
THE SAME SPIRIT THAT EXPLORERS
SHARE MAPS, HOPING TO SPEED EACH
OTHER'S JOURNEY, BUT KNOWING THE
JOURNEY WE MAKE WILL BE OUR OWN.'

GLORIA STEINEM ON MOTHERHOOD

Introduction

'Life on the planet is born of woman.'

ADRIENNE RICH

As we navigate the unfamiliar waters of motherhood, most of us will hit a reef or two that leave us stranded and in dire need of rescue. Yet these are the times at which we are least likely to ask for help and, unfortunately, the times we are most likely to be inundated with advice. I don't know about you, but I find advice incredibly difficult to take. It's not that I think I know it all, despite what my family may say, it's more that I usually don't know enough. I don't know enough to ascertain whether the advice is good or not, or even if it's good advice for someone else but not quite right for me. When I'm feeling unsure of myself and out of touch with my intuition, advice can be the extra element that sends me into a total spin. So one thing I promise here is no advice; I'm not qualified to, and do not intend to, tell you what you should do or how you can do things better. What I will offer is the same thing that has brought me so much clarity and joy over the years – the stories, tales, dilemmas and solutions of some of the other wonderful mothers in the world.

By now your child may be out of nappies; you've probably even popped the training pants back in the drawer. The last thing you need is another child-rearing manual, but that doesn't mean you no longer need guidance, inspiration or even a metaphorical shoulder to cry on. I breathed a sigh of relief when my youngest threw away her nappies, thinking that I must be out of the woods. I'd chosen to ignore the warning from my sister-in-law that although the physical grind of early childhood does disappear, the complicated emotional stuff is just beginning. Now that my children can all speak, go to the toilet and pour a glass of water for themselves, my role has changed. School, family, friendships and the 'poo-poo-penis-head' stage have all thrown me a curve ball or two and the shared laughter and rueful admissions of my girlfriends have helped me catch them. So now I'm going to repay the favour and share those stories with you. Some will make you laugh, others may be disquieting and the odd one will strike a chord in you and help show you the way through.

This book is by no means endorsed by anybody, and it is not intended to replace any of the excellent child-rearing manuals out there, several of which I found indispensable. It's not really even about our children, but about us, the women who, in the main, are bringing them up. Think of this book as a conversation with some of the mothers who are also working out how to do it their way.

Tackling motherhood as though it is a job can make it easier, but it can also make it harder. There's something disturbing about comparing your role as a mother with your role as an employee – surely bringing up our kids is something that we do out of love, that is unconditional, and about them and not us? In some ways this makes sense – if anything, motherhood is more of a vocation than a job; no pay, no leave and no tax-deductible perks. And like any vocation, this nurturing business is not something you can take a vacation from. Booking a weekend away sans kids may give you a break, but it doesn't mean you're suddenly not a mother. Try pulling that one off if the phone rings at 2 am just as you sway home from the bar by the pool and it's your mother on her way to a distant hospital with a vomiting, feverish child. You can try saying, 'Sorry, but I'm on annual leave and all caring duties have been fully delegated for the duration', but it won't get you very far. In fact, try saying it just to yourself and see what your reaction is. You'll find yourself in front of the mirror giving yourself a sharp talking-to should you even dare to think it. The second the phone rings at 2 am the carefree girl at the bar will be a distant memory as the mother inside you comes roaring back to the fore and you'll probably find you've finished packing all the bags before you've even had time to get off the phone. Once you've entered the hallowed halls of motherhood it all becomes a bit 'Hotel California' – you can check in any time you like but you can never leave.

So where does that leave you? I certainly didn't stop being me the day I became a mother, though I did lose myself for a little while. The birth of your first baby simply swallows you up and takes you into a different dimension. During the early months, or even years, you live in another place – you're a citizen of baby-land – until suddenly one day, you find you've been ejected, spat back out into the real world. You've made it through the wilderness and everyone is, hopefully, still in one piece, but mothering no longer consumes your every waking, and even sleeping, moment and you're faced with another tough transition. Now you have to work out how to be a mother and be you. You have to find out who you are all over again because no one goes through a shift as all consuming as becoming a parent and comes out the other side the same person they were. Your essence may be the same, but your thoughts, needs and feelings may well be very different.

If you're anything like me you may discover that you no longer even know what your needs are. You've spent so long catering to everyone else's needs that yours seem to be invisible. It's easy to run the schedule when you know that Tom needs new shoes, Sophie needs picking up at three to go to the doctor, Will needs to have a buddy over this Saturday and your mate needs a bit of your time. It's not so easy to consult the schedule to find out what you need, and when your needs do push their way in, claiming a slot on Wednesday afternoon, it can be really hard to not feel guilty simply for having them. If the schedule requires an emergency change and there's a clash between your coffee with Elle and Bertie's swimming class running late, who loses out? You wouldn't even consider cancelling the class just so you could have a coffee and a chat, would you? No matter how badly you need the break, it will automatically be rescheduled so that you can keep on running the family while you run yourself into the ground.

So one day you're going to find yourself standing there, just like the little boy at the counter, saying, 'What about me? It isn't fair'. And do you know what? That isn't bad, in fact it's actually very smart because the chances are that you are the captain of the ship and if you fall overboard, the ship may well sink. So when the time comes, and it will come, when you find that the person inside the mother comes pushing her way through shouting, 'Hey, can I have some bloody attention too, please?', it's your duty to listen to her and factor her in or you might just lose her altogether. Then your schedule will really go out the window as you cast about trying to find yourself again.

Which brings me back to mothering as a job, because in a strange way equating this business of rearing a child with whatever business you did before will make it easier to manage. Unless you were CEO of a multinational in your previous incarnation, the chances are that no one at work expected you to be God. The role you played in the workplace was defined and you knew what was expected of you and how to get it done. When you go about making a TV program you hire a range of people who specialise in certain aspects of the job – a cameraman, soundie, producer, researcher, writer, talent, editor and more. And you certainly wouldn't expect them to be interchangeable or any one of them to do it all on their own. But bring that squalling newborn home from the hospital and suddenly you really are playing God. Not only are your decisions a matter of life and death, but you're meant to be able to make them all on your own. Sure, at first you might have your partner there to consult with, but the chances are he'll be hopping off back to work before your nipples are tough enough and you're left on your own staring down the barrel of a newborn.

That's when it gets complicated, as if it wasn't to start with anyway and that's when you really have to work it out by yourself. There are only so many times you can ring your partner in a panic while he's in a meeting before it begins to sink in. When it comes to the nine to five, or maybe eight to eight, of bringing up baby, you're it. I still remember the first time my firstborn was really, really sick. Not just a little bit feverish with a bit of a cough and a faint but worrying rash around his mouth, but really, really scarily, uncontrollably vomiting sick. I literally looked around the bedroom in a panic, trying to spot the grown-up who would come along and sort this out for me. The shock when I realised that that grown-up was me, that the buck stopped here, has never fully left me. In a way it was more shocking than that first serious labour pain, the one that seemed to last for absolutely ever. This moment was the instant at which it really sank in that I had no choice but to grow up and get a serious handle on how to be a mother, and that I'd better be quick about it.

There's a myth that's responsible for more angst and depression among new mothers than any other single factor: the myth that being a mother comes naturally, that all you have to do is successfully breed and you will automatically know how to successfully mother. For most of us loving and caring come pretty naturally but the two are not synonymous with being a mother. They are only part of what it takes to bring up kids and on their own are definitely not enough.

What most of us lack when we are first hired are the skills required to do the job, the skills with which earlier generations did seem to come ready-equipped. I sometimes feel there is a line of mothers standing behind me, all the generations who seemed to learn how to mother at their own mother's knee. My great-grandmother died of tuberculosis when my grandmother was nine, and as the eldest daughter she was expected to step right into her mother's shoes. And step into them she did, raising her twin sisters and younger brother and cooking and cleaning for the whole family. It was an enormous task for a young girl, and not one that I'd wish on my daughter, but Grandma didn't need to learn any of the skills it took to run a family – she'd been her mother's apprentice since the day she was old enough. Families were larger and the extended family much more the norm. Children were expected to play an active role in family matters from a very young age and the skills they would need in later life were deliberately instilled. So my grandmother gave birth to my mother secure in the knowledge that she knew how to bring her up. I'm not entirely sure I'd use the same methods, but she had a confidence that I ached for in those early times.

But knowing how to bring up kids is more than just learning how to change nappies and feed them properly – it's more than just bringing up baby. I breathed a sigh of relief as I ticked each milestone off with my first child. And if I'm going to be honest with myself, and, believe me, I cringe at the memory, there was a little spark of triumph when milestones were reached early. It wasn't that I wanted to compete with other mothers or feel that my baby was smarter than theirs, well, not entirely anyway, it was because I felt as though I was getting an excellent KPI report at work and knowing I was still on the fast track. It wasn't even about my son, oh, the shame, it was about me and my fears that I was really out of my depth. There were two things that saved me from spiralling down the madness of the competitive mummy track. One was being stupid enough when it comes to contraception to have three babies in less than three years. Once I'd hit the point where my oldest was two years and nine months, my second 13 months and my third only three days old I had trouble even remembering my name, let alone being able to track their development.

'If you're not confused you're not paying attention.'

TOM PETERS

The second, and most important, thing that happened to me, the event that proved to be my salvation, was falling in with a group of absolutely wonderful women who all happened to have children around the same age as mine. Some I met through joining a mothers' group – the same dreaded mothers' groups I'd regarded with scorn pre-birth. Others I met in parks, at barbecues, because a mutual friend thought we'd hit it off, at work, in fact, all over the place. One of my most cherished friends I met in a carpark when we checked on each other's babies through the windows of the car. These women have made me laugh, kept me sane, helped me through some incredibly rocky situations and even been good enough friends to pull me up when I'm on the wrong track.

Not that I would ever be so stupid or arrogant to discount or discard my childless friends. They are all, to a man and a woman, fabulous, interesting, charming and stimulating people who have been generous enough to keep on including and inviting me despite my current tendency to run incredibly late, cancel at the last minute and be so out of touch with fashion it's embarrassing. But while these friends keep me in touch with the real world, it is my co-mothering girlfriends who have kept me afloat. They have offered something I could not have done without. Not advice (a sticky subject anyway), but empathy, compassion, a helping hand and an example to follow. They have been my saviours and so I dedicate this book to all the women doing what we try to do, to mother and to love with generosity, compassion and a healthy dose of trench humour.

'If love is the answer, can we rephrase the question?'

LILY TOMLIN

What I've tried to give you here is some of their stories, stories that are rarely heard but should be because they represent the reality of motherhood (and, yes, names have been changed to protect both the innocent and the guilty). Not everyone's reality will be the same, but for me the important thing about these stories is the way they highlight both our differences and our similarities. One of the great shocks for me was the way that producing heirs seemed to diminish my individuality in the eyes of the world. I was no longer a unique person with strengths, weaknesses and intriguing/irritating quirks, I was now a 'mother'. It's all very well being a revered archetype, but it doesn't help when it comes to working out how the hell to do something you have no experience at and are, frankly, pretty underprepared for. One of the things I found hardest was working out whether or not I was even normal.

'IN THREE WORDS I CAN SUM UP
EVERYTHING I'VE LEARNED
ABOUT LIFE: IT GOES ON.'

ROBERT FROST

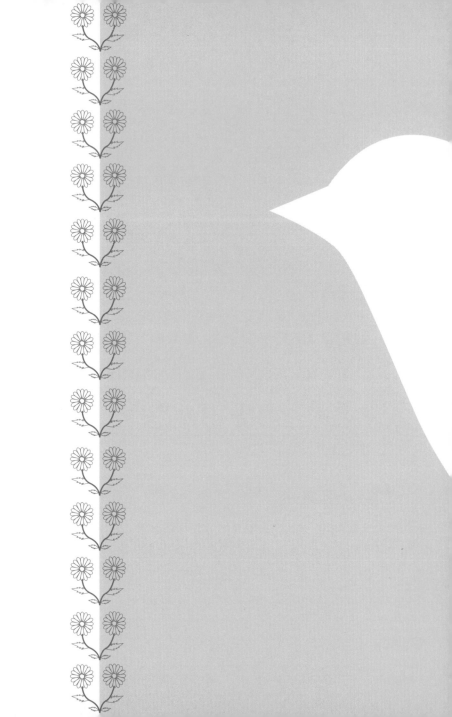

A mother is born

'LIFE IS RATHER LIKE A TIN OF
SARDINES – WE'RE ALL OF US LOOKING
FOR THE KEY.'

ALAN BENNETT

Over the hump

'Bite off more than you can chew, then chew it.'

ELLA WILLIAMS

What is the hump? It's the moment before you hit your stride, before you get your second wind. It's the hour before dawn, the last hurrah of pre-competence. It's the sinew-straining stretch when you think you cannot take another step or draw another breath. It's also known as the preschool years (which are, of course, also fabulous in their own right, but that's another story altogether).

When you start this great life game of bringing up babies it seems that each stage is somehow a discrete, finite block. When you are still incubating it's impossible to look past the birth with anything but the haziest of visions. No matter how hard those around us try to prepare us for life after birth our eyes remain firmly locked on what we see as the finishing line – the birth itself. Of course, that changes pretty swiftly once we get the baby home and discover that we've made a little person, not just a baby. Life quickly becomes consumed with feeding, changing, sleeping, wanting to sleep, washing, crying, needing to sleep, laughing, sobbing, desperately seeking sleep. Again we are immersed in the here and now and it seems that this stage of life will both last forever yet must also end, a bit like those final contractions. Except that, unlike labour, somehow you assume that once it ends you will just go back to being who you were before baby. None of this makes sense, but then the early days of child-rearing are not exactly the most rational time in most women's lives.

I spent the first few years thinking, 'Right, I'll just get through this bit, get this thing done, move on from this stage, and then ...' until one day I caught myself and thought, 'And then what?'. When I sat down and tried to work out what was this magical 'then' I was aiming for, I simply couldn't come up with an answer.

Recently I bumped into a friend of a friend on the street. This particular woman is an actress – gorgeous, articulate, interested and interesting. We know each other, but only to say 'Hi'. You know the kind of acquaintance: she acted in a show with an old school friend of mine, then we lived in the same street for a while – the kind of relationship where it would be rude not to say hello, but there's rarely anything else to add. So, the other day I was right at the end of my morning rush hour, one child dropped off at school, another at preschool and now the third safe and sound at day-care. All I had left to do was get to work, inhale a triple espresso and get down to it. I was fumbling in my scary, over-stuffed handbag searching for keys and when I say I bumped into Jane, I literally bumped into her. For once we had to say more than hello. First of all it was the whole, 'Sorry', 'No, I'm sorry', 'No, really, it was my fault' thing. Then a quick minute of, 'So, what are you up to, then?' and a brief, 'And how is Amanda these days?'.

Just as I was about to take my leave, Jane put a hand on my arm and asked me the strangest question. She said, 'How did you ever get around to doing it?' I paused and thought, 'Doing what? Washing my hair? Eating breakfast? Having a shower?' (all of which I'd managed to achieve that day). In the end I had to ask, only for Jane to say, 'Having children'. So I did what anyone would: rang work, said I'd be late and went for coffee.

It turned out that Jane, in her middling to late thirties, was seeing two different guys. One of them was employed, adoring and desperate for her to have his babies. The other was a whippersnapper of 22, gorgeous, irresponsible and amazing in bed. Jane felt like she was caught in a trap. To her, Mr Responsible offered the reality of a mature but possibly stultifying future. Surfer Boy offered good times and hot loving but the chance that she'd miss the mummy boat altogether. Jane's biggest problem was that she was ambivalent about having children fullstop, but afraid that one day, if she didn't have them, she would ultimately have to bear a loss that could not be borne. Jane seemed to think that if she could crack the code, she could make the right decision and that questioning me, understanding my motivation to reproduce, would help her untangle her desires. Problem was, for her at any rate, I had no idea why I'd had children.

Maybe it was an age thing, but when I got pregnant in my twenties, I didn't think about it, I just did it. Talking to Jane I began to think that, for me at least, that had been a good thing. The problem with the things she was asking was that, thoughtful as they were, they had no real answer. It was like a litany of rhetorical questions covering every element of her life: career, self, relationships, leisure, freedom, the works. So now she had me sitting in front of her, in her eyes a 'supermama', and frankly there was no way I could help. It's not easy trying to sell motherhood. Believe me, I tried, but the joys of mother-hood are so often intangible that communicating them can be a thankless task. I wish I'd had the gorgeous words given to me by a friend to put down in front of her:

'For a minute there I was going to forego having a baby because my partner did not want another child. I convinced myself that life without a child would be fine: we would have more money, more time, more freedom and pert everything. But a bottle of wine and a late night produced our son, and now I reflect, "What was I thinking? I could have missed all of this". Yes, I would have had all of those things but I would have missed out on this amazing thing that is happening to me – I have never been this in love. I love our son so much and am excited to see him each day. Nothing else matters now. Of course I would never have known, but I thank my lucky stars that it happened.'

It's hard for me to appreciate the headspace of someone struggling with the concept of parenthood. I always knew I would have children and I was lucky enough to mate young, so having a baby was just something that happened naturally. Besides, I've been doing it for so long now I can barely remember life before children. And I mean children; it's interesting that when people are struggling with the whole breeding question, what they talk about and imagine are babies. Babies are a massive shock to the system, they are time-consuming and bewildering and adorable and ephemeral. Babies become children in the blink of an eye and it's not the side-effects of having a baby that last, it's the side-effects of having children.

Sometimes I cringe at the memory of how censorious and judgmental I was prone to being in the days before I bred. I have an incredibly

'THERE ARE ONLY TWO LASTING
BEQUESTS WE CAN HOPE TO GIVE
OUR CHILDREN. ONE IS ROOTS;
THE OTHER, WINGS.'

HODDING CARTER

clear memory of being on a train from London to Oxford while I was pregnant with child one. I had miscarried twice before striking it lucky with my third pregnancy and I just knew that nothing as precious as this baby I was carrying existed anywhere. The train stopped at Didcott Parkway, a classic Victorian station set in divine countryside, with a view of four massive cooling towers. Into my carriage came a smartly dressed but obviously harried family of four. The younger child, a boy of about seven, kept up a constant commentary as they boarded, 'Look, Mummy, I'm carrying my case. Look, Mummy, I've put it on the rack. Look, Mummy, these seats are free. Look, Mummy, I'm sitting by the window'. With his classic little-boy haircut and clear English accent, I was very taken by him, and couldn't help smiling.

Then his mother snapped, 'For God's sake, James, could you just shut up for one minute!'. I was ridiculously shocked and wrote her off as an obvious harridan, uncaring and selfish, who clearly did not deserve to be a mother. Well, hang my head in shame if I haven't had to screech to a halt on the verge of spitting out the same words myself. The only thing that has stopped me is that crystalline memory of the horror I felt on the train. Now I just feel a different horror, at my callow younger self that saw women with children only as mothers, not as real people with busy lives and conflicting needs.

THE FAÇADE OF MOTHERHOOD

I swear that one of the things that can make those early years so tough is the way that, in public at least, your real self becomes invisible, masked by the façade of motherhood. Serenity is something I aim for but rarely achieve. There are days, and sometimes weeks, where I fear I'm developing a paranoia complex, because, apart from the obvious answer that the world is conspiring against me, there is no apparent reason why it is that everything that possibly could go wrong, does go wrong. My wonderful friend Danielle just snorts and says, 'Big deal, baby, that's life, get over it'. Thing is, I can get over it, it's just everyone else who can't. When I'm having a bad day, to me, I'm just having a bad day. From the reaction of complete strangers on the street, you'd think I was betraying the whole institution of motherhood. I sometimes wish I had a flyer I could hand out to anyone rude enough to 'tsk' as I rush past in the course of an unusually crappy morning. It would read something like this:

YES, I AM A MOTHER, AND YES, YOU DID JUST CATCH ME IN THE ACT OF:

A) STONILY IGNORING MY WAILING CHILD; OR

B) HISSING STERN WORDS OF WARNING; OR

C) SCREAMING HYSTERICALLY.

I APOLOGISE PROFUSELY FOR MY INABILITY TO BE ANGELIC AND SERENE AT ALL TIMES, BUT PLEASE BEAR IN MIND THAT IT IS ENTIRELY POSSIBLE THAT:

A) I AM LABOURING ON DESPITE HAVING A COLD THAT WOULD SEND THE CHILD-FREE SCURRYING BACK TO BED; OR

B) MY FATHER IS ILL, MY BOSS BAD TEMPERED AND MY BABY TEETHING; OR

C) I HAVE JUST DISCOVERED MY BEST FRIEND'S HUSBAND IS BEDDING HIS NUBILE YOUNG SECRETARY.

OF COURSE, IT'S ENTIRELY POSSIBLE THAT NONE OF THE ABOVE IS APPLICABLE TODAY, BUT ONE THING I CAN ASSURE YOU IS THAT

I AM ONLY HUMAN.

What has all this got to do with getting over the hump? The day I realised I no longer felt compelled to explain myself to all and sundry, that I, in fact, didn't give a flying fig what they thought of me, was the day I realised I had finally come to terms with my life as a mother. Settling into motherhood rarely happens overnight. Some of us are born to it and really do take to it like the proverbial duck. A few souls are so shaken by the changes in their life and their heart that they never again feel quite right. Most of us spend the first year or so reeling, often so consumed by daily reality we are oblivious to the momentous changes taking place inside. However it happened for you, the chances are you went through a period of confusion and fragility, a time when 'the slings and arrows of outrageous fortune' hit their target with alarming precision, leaving you shaken and unsure of who you were or what you wanted.

Circumstance plays an enormous role in shaping most women's early experiences of motherhood. I spent the first six weeks of my son's life in the cosiest situation imaginable. We were living in London when I got pregnant and I decided pretty quickly that I didn't want to do this for the first time with no back-up. Two days before the cut-off date for flying, and already enormous with child, I boarded a plane bound for Australia. I spent the last three months of my pregnancy wallowing in the pristine waters of Perth's Cottesloe Beach, setting off the occasional 'beached whale' alarm, and immensely happy. Two weeks before I was due, my husband joined us and when Tom was finally born, ten days late, we took him home to my parents' house. In retrospect, I can't believe how lucky I was. My dad cooked, my mum cleaned, my baby sister, only 17 at the time, would come in at 6 am to take Tom and let his shell-shocked parents sleep. After six weeks of heaven we flew back to London and, as you can imagine, the reality of looking after Tom all on my lonesome was a rude shock. My tan faded pretty fast in a grey London winter, but what lasted was my confidence. Bored, tired and frustrated I might be, only on occasion, of course, but I had the luxury of feeling like I knew what I was doing.

THE MUMMY MAFIA

It's remarkable that doing something that is supposed to come naturally can throw otherwise confident women into a spin. Being a long way from home can turn shifty ground into emotional quicksand. 'I was pregnant in Sydney, a long way from my home town of Perth,' says Lee, 'and a long way from the support network of family and old girlfriends. My partner had been retrenched just before the birth of the baby so we pretty keenly felt the need for support and hungrily took advantage of every little bit of help and advice going. I'd heard a lot about mothers' groups. They were this fantastic warm and comforting sorority of kindred souls, fabulous young urban mums recreating the sisterly and matronly bonds of another era, sharing wisdom and forging fantastic friendships that would be the bedrock of their social life and sanity for the years to come.

'So I rocked up for my first session, kind of trembling with anticipation. I think I knew from the first five minutes it would be a disaster. For a start, everyone else was wearing pristine white. Where did that come from? Did I miss the class that taught you how to pull off the languid summer look with an eight-week-old in tow? The community nurse was passing out a range of brochures on council services. As she displayed the childcare pamphlet she chuckled and said, "Although it's not as if any of you will need this info for a while yet."

'Right then, we were desperate for an income and so I had to get back to work. I timidly put my hand up and said, "Erm, excuse me, I do need that."

'A murmur actually ran around the room, and the woman sitting next to me said, "Oh gosh, I don't know how you could bear to part with him, they seem so little," like I was doing it for fun!

'Later, we moved on to sleeping and settling. Nothing could have prepared me for the outbreak of condemnation when I mentioned we were co-sleeping. Comments ranged from, "My husband would never allow it" to "Well, I guess if you want to, but personally, I could never take the risk." Well that was that, my reputation as a child-abandoning, risk-taking, hard-hearted mama was official.'

Lee acknowledges that her isolation and financial anxiety exaggerated her reaction to the perceived criticism of the group. 'I realise that these women were probably perfectly nice people and reacting from their own fear and anxiety about learning to be mums. But I guess this experience made me realise just how vulnerable I was to this kind of judgment and just how conservative much of the underlying social attitudes towards women as mothers still is.'

I don't know if I'd be as generous as Lee. My experience of mothers' groups is that they are as wildly varied as the women who comprise them. Woe betide the insecure girl who falls into a group of 'über-mamas'. Like chooks in the yard, or kids in the playground, there is a scary breed of mother out there who pecks the line into order in double-quick time. It's a funny old thing the 'anything-you-can-do' game, and the one-upmanship that comes with it can be rampant in the mummy mafia.

The thing that struck me time and time again while conducting the research for this book was the striking link between confidence and happiness. Whether the topic up for discussion was work, weaning or wedlock, confidence was the link. It didn't matter what decision the woman had made, what had led her there or what the general reaction to her choice was, the more confident she was that the decision she'd made was the right one for her, the happier she was. Almost all of the unfortunate breed of hardline mamas I've met have one thing in common, the desire to hide their own doubts at all costs, preferably by undermining you and proclaiming their own superiority from the rooftops.

THE TAO OF SELFISHNESS

'The history of all times, and of today especially, teaches that ... women will be forgotten if they forget to think about themselves.'
LOUISE OTTO

Making decisions based on your own needs can become incredibly fraught once you're responsible for meeting everyone else's needs as well. I can't count the number of times a girlfriend has started the story of doing something she wanted with the words 'I feel so guilty, but ...' Well, take a deep breath, remember who you are and begin to embrace the Tao of selfishness. This is lesson number one for finding your way out of the mire and over the hump.

'WHEN MY HUSBAND LEFT – EVEN NOW THOSE WORDS ARE SO DIFFICULT TO SAY – I WENT INTO A STATE OF TOTAL SHOCK. SOMEONE WHISKED THE KIDS AWAY AND I SPENT FOUR DAYS SHAKING, CRYING, HYPERVENTILATING AND WANTING TO DIE. I TOOK TWO FURTHER DAYS OFF WORK, THEN PULLED MYSELF TOGETHER AND GOT ON WITH IT. THREE WEEKS DOWN THE TRACK, MY FRIEND DEI SAT ME DOWN FOR A COFFEE AND SAID, "ALEX, THE TIME HAS COME FOR YOU TO STOP SAYING, 'OH MY GOD, WHAT THE FUCK HAPPENED TO MY LIFE?'. ACCEPT THAT IT HAS HAPPENED AND START ASKING, 'WHAT DO I WANT?'". I LISTENED, NODDING, AND THEN REALISED SHE WAS

WAITING FOR AN ANSWER. I CAST ABOUT AND OFFERED UP SOMETHING PATHETIC. "NOPE," SHE SHOOK HER HEAD, "THAT'S WHAT HE WANTS, WHAT DO YOU WANT?". I TRIED AGAIN, SAME RESPONSE. "NO, THAT'S WHAT THE KIDS WANT, WHAT DO YOU WANT?".

'I BURST INTO TEARS AND SAID, "GOD, DEI, I DON'T KNOW WHAT I WANT." IT WAS A SHOCKING REALISATION FOR ME THAT I'D LOST TOUCH WITH MYSELF TO THAT EXTENT.

'"WELL, YOU'D BETTER FIND OUT," SAID DEI. IT TOOK ME A SOLID WEEK OF THINKING TO WORK OUT WHAT I WANTED AND NEEDED, AND IT WAS THE BEST THING I COULD HAVE DONE. IT WAS LIKE DEI GAVE ME A PRICELESS GIFT.'

Officially employed or not, the chances are you're running the show. I love the statistics that litter the newspapers several times a year showing the average number of hours women and men spend on household tasks. They break it down into employed full time, part time and home duties, but one thing shines through every year. Regardless of the circumstances of a given couple, the chances are that the woman is doing three times as much housework and childcare as the man, whether she works outside the house or not. Three times! Twice as much, I could just about buy, but three times as much is outrageous. Put that together with the trend for huge houses with small gardens, and what you get is an even greater inequality in workload. How many households do you know where the woman takes care of the house and the man the garden? Bet they're loving the rise and rise of the McMansion, with its three bathrooms, home theatre and minuscule courtyard. Not that I want to get into the great housework debate, well, not in this chapter anyway, but it's the perfect way to illustrate the necessity for selfishness.

'Selfish' is a contentious word to use – the connotations are so negative – but it's hard to come up with a neat alternative. I could use a phrase like 'Taking your needs into account', but you try working that into a pithy sentence. It's tempting to coin a word like 'self-fulness' but not only does it not make sense, it's plain ugly. So for now, let's stick with 'selfishness' and redefine it to suit our needs.

Back to work it is, then, and whatever that means for you, I'm willing to bet it's a little more time-consuming and energy-sapping than you anticipated. Being captain of your ship doesn't just mean you are bound to go down with it should it sink, it means you're responsible for keeping it afloat in the first place.

> 'WHEN I AM STRONG, THEN I CAN DEAL WITH ANYTHING. IF I'M FEELING WEAK, I JUST FALL APART. IN ORDER TO BE STRONG, IT WAS ESSENTIAL I FIND THE TIME AND SPACE TO MEET MY OWN NEEDS. IT'S AMAZING HOW QUICKLY PEOPLE WILL ACCUSE YOU OF BEING SELFISH. I OVERHEARD ONE OF THE MUMS AT SCHOOL SAYING, "SHE'S JUST IN IT FOR HERSELF". I HAD A GIGGLE AT THAT ONE. YEAH, I'M PARTLY IN IT FOR MYSELF, IT'S MY LIFE AFTER ALL, BUT MEETING MY NEEDS MAKES ME HAPPY, AND WHEN I'M HAPPY I'M A GREAT MOTHER.'

So let's just accept that in these circumstances being selfish equates with doing anything that ostensibly benefits only you and just move right along.

You see, when it comes to running the show, anything you do that puts a spring in your step is ultimately going to work in your family's favour. Don't get me wrong, I'm not advocating that you spend your life ensconced on the sofa, eating chocolate, drinking wine and watching Johnny Depp movies. It might be fun for a day or two, but ultimately, you'll end up obese, alcoholic and frustrated, which is no good for anyone. What I'm saying is that you have a duty to look after yourself, to do things that make you feel good even if there's no apparent, immediate benefit for your family.

'EVERY THREE TO FOUR MONTHS I GO AWAY FOR THE WEEKEND WITH THE SAME GROUP OF GIRLFRIENDS. WE LIVE FOR THESE WEEKENDS AWAY AND SPEND AGES PLANNING THEM, WORKING OUT WHERE WE'LL GO, EMAILING EACH OTHER ABOUT SUITABLE WEEKENDS, TRAVEL TIME, WHO'S BRINGING DINNER AND WHO'S BRINGING WINE. ON THE SURFACE, THESE WEEKENDS LOOK PRETTY INDULGENT, AND I GUESS THEY ARE. WE DRINK, SLEEP, READ AND TALK AND THEN WE HEAD HOME TO OUR FAMILIES. LAST TIME WE WERE AWAY WE SPENT THE SATURDAY EVENING SITTING IN A SPA, DRINKING CHAMPAGNE, LOOKING OUT OVER THE MOUNTAINS AND GOSSIPING. I DON'T KNOW ABOUT THE REST OF THE GIRLS, BUT I'M THE BEST MUMMY IN THE WORLD WHEN I GET HOME. THOSE WEEKENDS AWAY ARE LIKE THE EQUIVALENT OF A REGULAR CAR SERVICE – THEY KEEP ME RUNNING.'

The key to staying on top is not just the big treats like weekends away or nights out, it's also about making time for the little things that soothe your soul. For me, it's reading. I can't remember a week when I didn't have a book on the go, and my idea of a nightmare is to be forbidden that escape into worlds beyond my daily scope. Occasionally, someone will say, 'I don't know how you find the time to read'. I assure them that if I didn't I'd probably be hospitalised, and that in order to do it I make a chain of little sacrifices. Sometimes those sacrifices affect the other members of my family; with a book in hand I'm not always 100 per cent available, but those little sacrifices are nothing compared to the diminished person I become if denied access to my fiction habit.

For as long as she can remember Sandy has needed a physical outlet for her energy. 'I'm just a bit hyper,' Sandy says. 'I need to work out in one form or another everyday or I'm a jittery mess. I run, I go to the gym and, most of all, I do yoga. I know it pisses my husband off. It's not a matter of principle, he doesn't believe that I should be there at all times, it's more a matter of logistics – for me to do my classes either requires him to get home early or we end up paying for a babysitter. For a while I argued with him, tried to justify why I needed to do it, and explain the benefits for everyone. Then I thought, "What is he, my father?" and decided to do it anyway. I'm not an idiot, I know what works for me and at the end of the day, the things that make me stronger work for my family.'

Sandy is right, she's not an idiot, and neither are you. So trust yourself, rediscover your needs and do the things that make you feel like you. Finding the confidence to be who you need to be and meeting your needs is the key step to getting yourself over the hump.

'PEOPLE SHOP FOR A BATHING SUIT WITH MORE CARE THAN THEY DO A HUSBAND OR WIFE. THE RULES ARE THE SAME. LOOK FOR SOMETHING YOU'LL FEEL COMFORTABLE WEARING. ALLOW FOR ROOM TO GROW.'

ERMA BOMBECK

Marriage and mates

'Love: a temporary insanity curable by marriage.'

AMBROSE BIERCE

Despite what the screaming tabloid headlines would have us believe, most children today are born into a family. That family may not reflect the cookie-cutter image that some people like to project as being the norm. Whether you are cohabiting, single or firmly wedlocked, young, old or Mrs Average, you are going to find yourself managing relationships alongside the one you have with your children. Maybe you are trying to bring up your kids and keep your marriage fresh, or you're on your own, living with your mum or thinking about bringing a new boyfriend home to meet the kids. Whichever way you cut it, you are going to run into the thorny side of intimacy.

Solving them is not always easy, especially when it seems like you and your mate are the only ones who aren't finding the whole shift in your lives one long period of bliss. It can be especially daunting when you become part of a gaggle of couples with kids. Everyone is kind and loving at parties and barbecues but it doesn't mean that life at home is always a bundle of fun nor does it mean it's a nightmare – most of us are just feeling our way through a natural realignment of our relationships. It's no great secret why this less-than-rosy period often remains hidden – when everyone else seems to be getting along just fine, you don't want to be the one to rock the boat or the odd one out, but the truth is that marriage with kids can be tough on love.

With so many possible permutations, finding the right word to use when writing about modern relationships is like a treasure hunt without clues. To make it easy for me, and let's face it, who doesn't want it easy, I've decided to stick with the word 'marriage', not only to save the slash key on my computer from burn-out, but because once you've had a baby with a man, assuming that's how you went about it, you are bound to him forever. Whether you live together or apart, love or hate him, share the joy of parenthood or the pain of separation, part of you will always be joined.

Marriage was the reason I wanted to write this book in the first place. When Tom, my first child, was born I bought and read every parenting book I hadn't already bought and read while still pregnant. I felt like I was an overflowing bottle when it came to changing nappies, dealing with crying and understanding the gastro-colic reflex, but where was the stuff about marriage? I knew that I loved my husband, in fact, I'd loved him since I was 15 (secretly and pathetically for the first six years) and I didn't feel that having his child was going to change that, but I was a little bit scared that it might. So I went back to the books, looking for a clue, something that would help me understand what having children does to a marriage. And weren't they helpful – a whole line, and sometimes even an entire paragraph, saying, 'Don't forget to find time for you and your partner'. Great, I suddenly felt like a stranger to myself, saw my husband through different eyes and that was the best they could do? In my maddest moments, my marriage felt to me like something made of glass, beautiful and precious but incredibly easy to break, and I needed help.

Everything changed inside me the night I gave birth to our first child – from the way I saw the world to the way I felt about myself – but I was somehow still the same person, especially from the outside. I had a sneaking suspicion this was going to make life pretty interesting and that it was possible I was going to be a tiny bit difficult to live with. Not that I felt it was all bad, far from it. I'd gaze at this little baby we'd made, who was, of course, the most beautiful baby ever born, and then gaze at my husband who was, of course, the most beautiful man in the world. At times it was so lovey-dovey in our household that it was almost sickening.

But at nights it was a different matter altogether. I'd say it took me only two weeks to learn to hate hubby during the night. The night-time feeds led to incremental resentment as I was most definitely not one of those women who found them a sacred time of comfort. I love my sleep, I always have, and I hated being woken at night. Babies and night feeds, stinking nappies and scattered toys are only the beginning of parenthood. So it follows that babies are only the beginning of the changes in your marriage.

'MICK AND I WERE CHILDHOOD SWEETHEARTS, SO EVEN THOUGH RUBY WAS BORN WHEN I WAS ONLY 26, WE'D ALREADY BEEN

TOGETHER FOR TEN YEARS AND THEY'D BEEN TEN REALLY GOOD YEARS. THINGS WERE STILL GOOD AFTER RUBY; THE THREE OF US MADE A REALLY GOOD UNIT. BEN WAS BORN JUST 13 MONTHS AFTER RUBY AND SUDDENLY THINGS WEREN'T SO HOT ANY MORE. HE WASN'T DIFFICULT OR ANYTHING, BUT LIFE JUST SEEMED SO MUCH HARDER. I WAS REALLY TIRED ALL THE TIME AND FOR THE FIRST TIME EVER, MICK AND I JUST FOUGHT CONSTANTLY. I WAS STRESSED AND SCATTERED AND SCARED AND DIDN'T KNOW HOW TO HANDLE THE CONFLICT WITH MICK 'COS IT HAD JUST NEVER HAPPENED BEFORE. THEN ONE NIGHT, MICK MADE ME A CUP OF TEA, SAT ME DOWN AND SAID, "JO, NO MATTER HOW BAD THINGS ARE NOW, NO MATTER WHAT HAPPENS NEXT, IF WE BOTH JUST AGREE TO STICK IT OUT THROUGH THE NEXT FIVE YEARS, EVERYTHING WILL BE GOOD." IT WAS SUCH A SIMPLE THING TO SAY, BUT SUCH A MAGIC THING. IT DIDN'T MEAN THAT LIFE WAS SUDDENLY A FAIRYTALE, IT JUST MEANT THAT I HAD SOMETHING TO HANG ONTO, SOMETHING THAT MADE ALL THE EVERYDAY CRAP SO MUCH EASIER TO HANDLE.'

I figured that if I was going to be audacious enough to commit my thoughts and opinions on marriage and motherhood to paper it might be a good idea to make sure that I knew what I was talking about. Being ill-informed and prejudiced doesn't usually get in the way of a strongly held opinion, especially after a couple of glasses of white, but being tipsy at a party is one thing and writing a book another thing altogether. So I decided to get organised and do some research.

First I rang my mum, then my sister and then my girlfriends. Then I got serious. I decided that if I was going to have any kind of authority at all I needed to speak to as many different mothers as was humanly possible, especially mothers I didn't know. So I got really modern and started a viral email campaign. I sent a list of questions to a bunch of girlfriends (actually, to every female who's ever given birth and crossed my path) and asked them to send it on, like one of those annoying chain letters, except this letter actually asked the recipient to do some work. The emails spread across the world like ripples in a pond. Well, across Australia and all the way to the UK and US. There were a couple of questions on love and marriage along the lines of 'What do you want?' and most of you seem to want the same things: companionship, support, respect, affection and love. Oh yes, and two of you wanted sex, or at least two of you still had the energy to think about sex in the abstract as well as perform it. Most of all, it seemed like women still wanted to be with the man they'd fallen in love with in the first place, not all of the time, just access to him on the odd occasion.

THE LIFE RAFT

'Tim and I were over the moon when Harry was born,' remembers Rose. 'We took him with us everywhere we went, and I mean everywhere – dinner, movies, football games – we even took him to a world music concert when he was seven days old. It was beautiful; we were there for my dad's birthday and one grandparent after the other rocked him in their arms while this incredible music sang out over the park. Then Leo was born only 18 months later. We were lucky, he was another easy, beautiful baby and we still seemed to be fairly portable. It was more work, but the boys still came with us everywhere we went.

'Then my mother came to stay with us; we were living in London and she came for several weeks. After a couple of nights Mum asked me if I could even remember the last time Tim and I had gone somewhere on our own. I could; it was two nights before I went into labour with

Harry. Mum insisted that it was time for us to find out how to be a couple again, that if our lives revolved around the boys (her words) we'd risk losing each other. I got quite defensive and upset, told her that everything was wonderful and this was how families did things these days. Mum said, "I'm not suggesting you go back to Victorian times, I just think you need to go on a date with your husband." So we did; we decided to go to the movies and Tim picked me up on the way home from work. Mum had to push me out of the door as I was so nervous about leaving the boys for the first time. She pointed out, with a touch of acid in her tone, that if she'd managed to raise the four of us she was probably capable of putting her grandsons to sleep.

'As soon as I got into the car I realised that I wasn't just nervous about leaving Harry and Leo, I was actually nervous about being alone with Tim. Driving there was like being on a first date and I was glad we were going to a movie as I actually didn't know what to say to him – somehow filling him in on a day packed with mashed banana and a trip to the park didn't feel quite right. Even after we'd taken our seats I still felt shy. Then Tim took my hand and suddenly, I just felt weird. Not uncomfortable, just weird. Then I realised that what I was feeling was love, and desire, and that I hadn't felt either for a while.

'After the movie we went to a noisy, smoky, grotty bar that was decidedly non-child-friendly and it felt bloody wonderful. We talked for hours and got so drunk (compared to the usual glass and a half) that we had to get a taxi home. After telling Mum we'd be in by 11, we rolled home at 2 am, giggling and shushing each other. Even with the hangover it was worth it. It made it clear to both of us that we'd stopped being Tim and Rosie when we were together and started just being Mum and Dad. It's so easy to lose sight of the person you love in the middle of your average family storm and our dates have become our life raft.'

MAKING WHOOPEE

Dates don't do it for everyone, but for many of us they are an important ingredient in the glue that holds a marriage together. And we all know where dates lead, or at least where they're meant to, and that's sex. Not that I'm obsessed with sex, or at least not all of the time, but I find it fascinating that sex in marriage gets so little airtime when it was part of the reason for it in the first place. Not that we live in a time when you have to get married to have sex; some of our mothers, and most definitely their mothers, did – and didn't that lead to a lot of fun divorces? But few of us bother to marry a man we don't want to have sex with, and even fewer breed within the confines of a platonic relationship. Yet somehow the outcome of all that fertile fun can be a depressingly philosophical relationship.

I plucked up the courage to push the sex angle a little harder. I tried to be really upfront and asked a couple of girlfriends, 'So what do you think of sex and marriage?' Problem was no one gave me an answer that was even vaguely printable. So I found a more subtle way to work it into the interviews. The results were incredibly varied but one thing was clear – sex mattered. Some felt they were expected to have too much sex, some weren't getting enough and a few weren't getting any. For some, sex was an incredibly important part of their relationship both before and after babies and others felt that becoming a mother had changed their sexual desires and their relationship with their body. Sex was an especially delicate issue in some relationships; where, when, why and how were all bones of contention. In others, it was the who – sex is never thornier than when someone is having sex with the wrong person. From third-degree tears to affairs, once the sex monster was out of the closet, everyone had something to say.

Most people are strangely uneasy about the combination of mothers and sex – my husband doesn't even like me to utter the two words in the same sentence, especially if I'm talking about *his* mother. It seems to have escaped his notice, at least in the bedroom, that I am now a mother. I sometimes wonder if it would be the end of our sex life if he put two and two together.

One arena where many women feel they cease to exist as sexual beings is in the examining room of their obstetrician. In some ways that is at it should be – most of us do not lie down on the couch feeling like a hot mama, and any obstetrician who suggested we were would soon hear the chilly tones of a disciplinary tribunal. But there is no escaping the fact that motherhood is intrinsically linked with women as sexual beings. While many babies are now born via IVF, few of us seek it out before trying the old-fashioned method of procreation. Yet many of the women I spoke to, especially those who suffered physical complications during labour, felt that when it came to the effect of those complications on their sex life there was a resounding silence.

Sometimes the physical ramifications of giving birth have a serious effect on a woman's sex life, and when this happens it may complicate an already difficult adjustment. When Will, number two for me, was 12 hours old, the nurse stopped by my bed to ask what I was planning to do about contraception. I looked at her incredulously, having just given birth to an 11-pound (5 kg) baby, and said, 'Contraception? I'm never having sex again!'. But of course, I did (I conceived number three only four months later) and once I'd got through the weirdness of 'the first time', things kind of went back to normal.

But for women whose sexuality has been radically affected by pregnancy and birth, whether physically or psychologically, the

'I THINK MEN WHO HAVE A
PIERCED EAR ARE BETTER
PREPARED FOR MARRIAGE.
THEY'VE EXPERIENCED PAIN
AND BOUGHT JEWELLERY.'

RITA RUDNER

changes in their sex life can have ramifications for the whole relationship. One woman who was unable to reach orgasm as a result, she believes, of a caesarian section, found that it had an unexpectedly negative effect on the way she felt about her husband. 'I'd always thought we had a really good sex life and that it was an expression of how deeply we loved each other,' says Jo. 'Then, after Katie was born, I just couldn't have an orgasm. At first I assumed that it was too soon after the caesar and it would just take time. Then I thought it must be psychological. Finally, after about 18 months, I went to see my doctor about it. Eventually, she said it was possible that the caesarian section had resulted in nerve damage that had "impaired my sexual function" and that was it. The problem was that it wasn't just the doctors who didn't seem to care, but my husband as well. It just didn't really trouble him, in fact, he wanted sex all the time anyway and didn't seem too worried that it did nothing for me. In the end I felt as though I was just servicing him and I started to wonder if the whole "star-crossed lovers" thing was just a figment of my imagination.'

For some women, problems in the bedroom can lead to a strengthening of their marriage as a whole. Lydia suffered a third-degree tear while delivering her first child and while the tear ultimately healed, after a year of medical assistance including the restitching of the scar, it took a lot longer for her to feel comfortable having sex. 'Sex had always been a huge part of our relationship and a big part of my life before I even met John. I felt really comfortable about liking sex, and we went out of our way to have as much sex as possible before Gabriel was born. I couldn't believe it when I tore like that, it was just horrendous. It took ages to heal and even then I just wasn't comfortable. It wasn't just a physical thing, I felt as though the birth had changed my body and therefore changed who I was as a woman. And, to be honest, I was scared about how John would react to me not wanting to have sex. It's funny because he's been so amazing. He still wants to have sex, but he's been slow, kind and gentle and it's made my love for him so much deeper and more real. Sometimes I want to talk to my girlfriends about how much his attitude has meant to me, but then I find most of them don't want to talk about sex, which makes me think that we're not alone when it comes to finding it hard after babies.'

'The most important thing a father can do for his children is to love their mother.'

THEODORE HESBURGH

AFFAIRS OF THE HEART

Even harder to navigate than sexual difficulties are affairs. When I was a teenager I'd look at my parents' friends and see frosty marriages, affairs, alcoholism, workaholism and all kinds of different problems. Not that they were a particularly dysfunctional lot (though at the time I thought they were), plenty of them had good marriages and wonderful lives. It's more that what seemed to me to be specific to these 'old' people is actually scarily normal. Time takes the tender glow off life in general, not just marriage, and it seems to me that a lot of people stumble through this midlife time trying to get it right, and sometimes messing up big-time. Few things throw a spanner into a relationship like an affair.

'I'm certain I caught my husband just before he had an affair,' says Louisa. 'He'd had a big night out with his colleagues and forgotten to take his phone to work with him. So I dropped it at the office and said to the receptionist, "How was last night?". She was raving about how mad it'd been, everybody really pissed and singing karaoke. I laughed and said I couldn't imagine Andrew singing karaoke. The second she looked confused I just knew. "Oh, Andrew wasn't there," she said. "He had to take a client out instead, poor bugger." Poor bugger, my arse! I'm on stepmother number three at the moment and I can promise you that when a man starts lying to his wife about his whereabouts it's about another woman.'

Of course it's entirely possible that the odd white lie is not automatic confirmation of an affair. We all have reasons for wanting to operate in private from time to time, but Louisa was convinced her instinct was right. 'It would have been prime time for him to have an affair. I was still breastfeeding, worn out and probably hard work, so when some slim Little Miss Tarty Pants comes into view, she's going to look good compared to you. The reason it's such a betrayal is that you were like that once too, before you got bogged down with the babies. So what if you're unattractive for a couple of years?'

Louisa won my admiration with her willingness to take decisive action. There was no agonising and reasoning for her. 'I went home, called him and told him he had half an hour to get home if he wanted to make it before the locksmith got here. Andrew had a staff of 110 at that stage and it was a 40-minute journey in good traffic, but I knew I needed to give him a huge shock if I wanted to stop this thing in its tracks. He was ten minutes late, but the locksmith was 20.'

Not every affair equals the end of the marriage, and sometimes they are a symptom of the tricky act of living life rather than simply a sign of a rotten marriage. A recent high-profile marriage ended up in the papers with tales of fights, affairs and AVOs. When asked about it the wife talked about the strain that the suicide of her husband's son had placed on their marriage and life in general. When things get really tricky, and at some stage they will for most of us, even the best marriages can start to unravel and sometimes even good people do bad things, including having affairs.

Amy had to deal with a full-blown affair, one that came as a massive shock, but she decided from the very beginning that, if it was up to her, the marriage would survive. 'After eight years and three kids our marriage hit a rocky patch. In fact, we went from sailing through the flats to screaming up the Himalayas overnight. My cosy life became a sordid year of lying, affairs, betrayal and heart-rending pain. Friends, especially single friends, kept saying, "Just give up", "Get rid of him" and "Enough already, are you a bloody doormat?" But I had to hang in there, not just for the kids, but because of the voice inside me that insisted that this wasn't right, that he still loved me and that what was happening made no sense. There's no point in going into the details unless you've got all year, but let's just say that somehow we hung in there and came out the other side.'

Not everyone would want to stand firm through a storm of betrayal, but Amy is adamant that she did the right thing. 'I look at marriages that have lasted 40 years and I can't believe that at some stage most of them didn't have to work through something horrendous. For all the pain we went through I truly believe that one day it will just be something that happened once ten years ago.'

Marriages do get messy sometimes and it's not always the man who has the affair. Several women were painfully honest with me about the affair (or affairs) they have had during their marriage, and the reasons for having them. It's not a massive surprise to discover that the link between the women I spoke to was the need to feel loved and desired. Nor is it a massive leap to assume that this need lies behind affairs of the heart for most men and women. There is no real excuse for betrayal, but understanding can be a step towards healing, especially if you can find a way to hold 'understanding' separate from condoning. Sociopaths, sexual predators and the smoothly amoral lurk among us, but when a supposedly wedlocked partner goes looking for love in all the wrong places, it's usually a sign that something is missing. Whatever that 'something' may be, whether it is fair or right, most people who stray into infidelity are seeking a taste of it; of the 'something' they feel they are missing.

'I WAS SO ANGRY WITH NICK; WE'D BEEN THROUGH A HORRENDOUS TIME FINANCIALLY AND I FELT, RIGHTLY OR WRONGLY, THAT IT WAS HIS FAULT. FOR THE PAST YEAR THE ANGER HAD BEGUN TO SWALLOW UP ANY OTHER EMOTION I MIGHT HAVE FELT, AND IT GOT TO THE POINT WHERE I JUST COULDN'T BEAR TO BE IN THE SAME ROOM AS HIM. I STARTED GOING OUT ALL THE TIME, HEADING OFF AS SOON AS HE GOT BACK FROM WORK AND GOING TO THE PUB AND THEN ON TO A CLUB. WHEN I MET CHARLIE I KNEW STRAIGHTAWAY THAT I WANTED TO LEAVE NICK AND BE WITH HIM. HERE WAS SOMEONE WHO MADE ME FEEL LIKE A WOMAN AGAIN, NO, LIKE A GIRL. WHEN I TOLD NICK I WANTED TO LEAVE HE WAS TOTALLY SHOCKED, HE REALLY DIDN'T SEE IT COMING. HE DECIDED THAT THE LAST THING HE WANTED WAS FOR HIS FAMILY TO BREAK UP AND HE FOUGHT LIKE A MADMAN TO FIX THINGS. IT TOOK A YEAR FOR ME TO COME AROUND, A YEAR OF COUNSELLING AND FIGHTING AND LEAVING AND COMING BACK. NOW I LOOK BACK AND THINK, "THANK GOD HE DID THAT FOR ME, FOR US. I NEARLY MADE THE BIGGEST MISTAKE OF MY LIFE."'

Making your way back from pain and betrayal is not an easy task. It's also an unfashionable way to deal with a fractured relationship. When my marriage hit a snarly point the message I got loud and clear, both personally and culturally, was 'Walk away'. There is a strong school of thought that says if your relationship is causing you pain it's no good for you and should therefore be disposed of. While I understood the sentiment behind this, and the friends who advised me to jump ship were doing so out of concern, it just didn't feel right to me. I saw my marriage as being damaged but still valuable and my instinct was to do everything I could to restore it to its former state. As I discovered, once you've gone down such a scary path, there's no returning to a state of innocent, wedded bliss, but that doesn't mean you can't make something even stronger. We did find our way through, and sometimes it seems that the glue we used to put the marriage back together is even stronger than the one that bonded us together in the first place.

'A successful marriage requires falling in love many times, always with the same person.'
                                        MIGNON MCLAUGHLIN

Dealing with the aftermath can be as difficult as making your way through the initial morass. Judy went through the pain of a marriage break-up six years ago and sometimes finds the pain still fresh now. 'I still have the odd cry, though it's nothing like it was. The break-up was hideous but I was running so scared that, in a way, the time flew past. Then when the mess subsided and we reconciled, the adrenaline deserted me and I just crashed. While trying to appear serene and competent inside I felt I was drowning in fear. I couldn't let go of the pain and hurt over what had happened and I was consumed with worry and anxiety about the future. Then one day I was driving home from work and listening to an interview with a man who had been in exile from his home country for 20 years. He was talking about happiness and how unhappy he'd been for every one of those years until, one day, it hit him that he had got time wrong. That every minute of every day he was either sad about the past or worried about the future, but never stopped to think about the present. His words struck such a chord that I sat there at the lights, put my head on the steering wheel and started to sob.

'That night in bed, I was lying there trying to pretend, as I did every night, that I wasn't on the verge of hysteria. My head was churning with painful memories and whenever I managed to put them away I would be hit with a surge of anxiety. My fear was that the future would be worse than the past because it would all happen again and the only thing that could be worse than the first betrayal would be another. Then, suddenly, I remembered the words I'd heard that afternoon and I stopped to see if I was even capable of knowing how I felt about the present. I let myself feel the warmth of holding Dan's hand, the peace of knowing that the kids were asleep, even the fact that Dan's steady breathing made me feel safe. Suddenly I knew that right then, in that minute, I felt happy. It wasn't a magic cure, but it was a step forward, a tool I could use to rebuild my life. Allowing myself to relax and feel happy, even just sometimes, helped put the past and the future into perspective. It let me finally begin to be able to talk to Dan about what had happened and about my fears without flying into a rage or collapsing into tears. And most of all, it taught me that it is okay to trust in and value the present as something distinct from that which has been and that which is still to come.'

Staying together is not always the solution. 'I just didn't feel loved any more,' says Anita. 'I felt as though our marriage had become this emotional black hole that had sucked all of the life out of me. We tried everything, counselling, time alone together, putting up with it, the works. But I just got unhappier and unhappier. I left Jeff in my mind long before I left him for real. He says now that he didn't really believe I'd go through with it until I did. I still don't know if I'm happier; it's only been six months and the emotional mess is still fresh.'

Anita found herself painted as the scarlet woman when she started a relationship only months after leaving Jeff. 'What people didn't understand was that we had been separate people for years. Friends and family only see what they want to see, and at first, I got really defensive 'cos it was all, "Oh, Anita's left Jeff for another man". Then I thought, let them think that if it makes it easier for them to understand. I know the truth and that's what matters.'

Now I'm going to moralise for a moment. I did say I'd give no advice but lots of opinions and I just happen to have one very strong opinion on this whole topic. It goes something like this: just because you are married and unhappy it does not necessarily follow that you are unhappy because you are married. Until death do us part is no longer laid down in stone, but I believe you owe it to yourself to first try really hard to work out if your unhappiness has another cause. Do everything you can to make yourself happy first. Then if you still can't handle the marriage, you can walk away clear in the knowledge that you couldn't be happy within it.

Of course, not every marriage gets so dramatically shaky; some are worn away by the erosion of daily life, others seem to stay strong no matter what. So what's the secret ingredient in those rock-solid marriages? I don't know, if I did I'd be a relationship guru, but there were some constants that emerged from the interviews. One was the level of support within and without the marriage. Family support can get a relationship through a minor squall while pressure from the wider clan can drive a marriage onto the rocks. Compatible views on children, acceptable behaviour and life in general seemed to be the bedrock of some relationships. Where beliefs were in harmony there seemed to be less conflict and a greater willingness to ride out the storms of life. But the most important thing to most of you was friendship. Without friendship marriage seems to founder once kids erode the remaining layer of romance.

Here it got tough again. I mean, how do you quantify friendship? It doesn't have to mean being in agreement on, well, anything, really. Nor is it about being in love, or about admiration or respect. If anything, friendship in a marriage seemed to revolve around the same thing as friendship in general – liking each other. No great revelation perhaps, but it kind of was for me. There have been moments in my marriage, only moments, when I haven't necessarily liked my husband, or for that matter, myself, but love has got me through the day. But could I have loved him if I really didn't like him? When the love fades, how do you get through if you don't like each other? All of the women who reported being happy in their marriage had one thing in common – there was one activity, no matter how trivial, that both of them actively looked forward to doing together and that most definitely did not involve the children.

'SOME OF MY GIRLFRIENDS COMPLAIN ABOUT BEING GOLF WIDOWS, BUT IN OUR HOUSEHOLD IT'S THE CHILDREN WHO ARE GOLF ORPHANS. EVERY SECOND WEEKEND, WITHOUT FAIL, PETE AND I PLAY 18 HOLES TOGETHER WHILE THE KIDS SPEND A DAY WITH THEIR GRANDPARENTS. IT'S SUCH AN IMPORTANT TIME FOR US THAT IT'S ALMOST BECOME SACROSANCT. I EVEN PLAYED THE DAY BEFORE I GAVE BIRTH TO MY SECOND KID BECAUSE I KNEW I'D HAVE TO TAKE SIX WEEKS OFF AFTERWARDS. IT'S SO PEACEFUL ON THE GREEN; WE ALWAYS PLAY ALONE AND HAVING THOSE HOURS TOGETHER GIVES US TIME TO JUST

HANG OUT. IF THERE IS SOMETHING MAJOR WE NEED TO TALK ABOUT, WE KNOW WE'VE GOT TIME TO WORK IT THROUGH, SO IT REALLY TAKES THE PRESSURE OFF. MOST OF THE TIME, THOUGH, WE DON'T REALLY TALK ABOUT ANYTHING, IT'S MORE ABOUT JUST BEING TOGETHER AND DOING SOMETHING THAT WE BOTH LOVE. IT'S GREAT FOR THE KIDS, TOO. MY MUM TAKES THEM ONE FORTNIGHT AND PETE'S PARENTS THE NEXT, SO THEY GET SPOILT ROTTEN TWICE A MONTH.'

Some mad friends of mine cook together (a recipe for divorce in my kitchen), others sail, some love a trip to the movies. For us it's lazy Sunday mornings reading the papers and drinking coffee. They're not easy to come by, but I usually manage to beg or bribe about four a year. Whatever it is, that shared time goes such a long way towards keeping the friendship going in a marriage, and friendship really can be the bond that matters.

'Marriage is our last best chance to grow up.'

JOSEPH BARTH

'IN EVERY CONCEIVABLE
MANNER, THE FAMILY IS LINK
TO OUR PAST, BRIDGE TO
OUR FUTURE.'

ALEX HALEY

In-laws and outlaws

'Happiness is having a large, loving, caring, close-knit family in another city.'

GEORGE BURNS

Unless you hook up with an orphan, at some stage you are going to be dealing with in-laws. It can seem quaint, looking back, at the nerves that accompanied meeting them for the first time, in the days when you were just the new girlfriend. Maybe they loved you, maybe they didn't, maybe you thought they were fascinating or even fascinatingly awful. And how did it go when you took him home for an initial appraisal? Did it go surprisingly well or was it buttock clenchingly awful? Or even worse, just boring? Did it make you reassess him, or your parents, or even yourself? However it went, it's likely that it seemed like a big deal and you had no way of knowing how much of a bigger deal it would ultimately become.

Creating your own family has a knock-on effect on the dynamics of your whole extended family. It can bring you closer together or exacerbate existing rifts, but the chances are it will lead you to re-evaluate your family life to date. Hands up if you've ever stood in front of the mirror and sworn that no matter what, you would never turn into your mother. Mmmm, and how long was it before that first motherism slipped from your blameless lips? Personally, I swore I'd never say 'Because I said so', now I just swear by it. Still, I'm not my mother, my mother-in-law, or even, my stepmother-in-law (when did it get so complicated?), but I am their heir in the generation game and all of them play an enormous role in my experience of being a mother.

One of the questions I asked any woman brave enough to talk to me for the book was: 'How has having children changed your relationship with your in-laws?'. As you can imagine, the replies came flooding in. They ranged in tone from, 'Great, they live 10 000 kilometres away' to 'Oh my God, where do I start?' to 'I can't even begin to tell you how amazing they've been'. Then one of my girlfriends said, 'What's with the in-laws question? Everybody knows about in-laws, but what about the way it changes your relationship with your own parents?'. What Sam had done in that one brief comment was lay out my own prejudices for examination. Because my relationship with my parents is relatively simple and, if anything, enhanced, by giving them grandchildren, my automatic focus was on the, for me, infinitely stickier situation of getting along with the in-laws. Not that I want to slag off my in-laws, especially not in print (and not to imply that my in-laws aren't fabulous people because, for the record, they are), but it's fair to say that getting along with them has been a more complex undertaking for me than getting along with my own parents. The fact that that complexity is simply a matter of comparison didn't prevent me from developing a prejudice that infected my questionnaire.

PARENTS THROUGH THE PRISM
OF MOTHERHOOD

There's nothing like moving up through the generations to give you a greater insight into your parents as people, especially your mother. For some, this is a humanising, healing moment as seeing their parents as complex, fallible people can be the first step to assuaging the hurts of childhood. For Bridget, her own difficulties were the catalyst for finally building a bridge between herself and her mother.

'My parents were some of the last of the "Ten-pound Poms" and I would have been one of the youngest,' says Bridget. 'They moved from the Midlands to Australia when I was only four months old. You know, it was just a piece of family history I grew up with, one of the puzzle pieces that make up your life. I'd never stopped to think about what it might actually have meant for me as a baby or for my mother.

'Then, when I had my daughter, I found myself living in the States with only my husband for support. His parents are both dead, and mine were still living in Australia and, my God, was I in it on my own. One night, Brad was still at work, Darcy was only eight weeks old and really colicky, and I just started crying. Once I started, I couldn't stop, so I put her in her cot, left her to scream, curled up on the bed and let it go. After a while, I realised that I wasn't just crying because I was tired or alone or any of those things, it was more as though I was in mourning.

'When I found out I was pregnant, I really wanted it to be a boy. My mother and I had always had such a distant relationship, completely different to the way she was with my brother. I just thought that things were harder for mothers and daughters and assumed I'd be able to love a boy better. That night, when all the tears poured out, I realised I was grieving for myself, for the place I was in, and for the mother I never really had. I felt I was a crap mother and it must be genetic, that I really was just like her. But as I lay there feeling sorry for myself it slowly dawned on me that the one thing Mum and I really had in common was the isolation we'd suffered when our first baby was born. Maybe, I thought, the reason I was finding it so hard to bond with Darcy was because I felt so completely alone, and if that was the case for me, what had it been like for Mum? At least I had email to keep me connected to friends at home; she didn't even have a phone until I was nearly one.

'It wasn't like a magic bullet that made everything in our relationship perfect, but starting to understand what it must have been like for her, helped me see everything in a more compassionate light. There wasn't anything intrinsically bad about either of us, it's just that sometimes life is really hard. She'd suffered, and then I'd suffered, but it was like realising that meant Darcy didn't have to suffer too.'

I found that having my own children made my relationship with my parents more solid and much more real than it had been. There was something about the love I felt for my babies that connected me to the love they felt for me and my siblings. It also made it so much easier to see them as individuals: loving, special, real and fallible. Few of us make it through our twenties without finding our parents responsible for everything we don't like about ourselves. Unfortunately, it doesn't take long in life after birth to realise that if that is truly the case we are all up shit creek. Children are really just a blind experiment. Not one of us actually knows what we are doing once we've delivered them into the world and we therefore just kind of make it up as we go along. I wouldn't bake a cake without a tried-and-tested recipe and it's kind of scary to realise that there isn't one for bringing up baby.

'My relationship with my mum was so much better before I had Damon. It makes me sad that I'm actually glad she lives in another state. Every time she suggests a visit I get excited, but once she actually gets here I can't wait for her to go. It's not that she does anything majorly awful, and she's great with the kids, but she just can't stop herself making these cutting little comments. She came to stay after Johnny was born and I really needed the help. I had a preschooler and a baby and even though I was meant to be on leave, I'd agreed to run one project from home. I felt totally run-down, I looked like shit and I just needed some help.

'Three days into her visit I was having a particularly nasty day and was in tears by lunchtime. So Mum took the boys off to the supermarket with her and I grabbed a quick nap. By the time they got back I'd even had time for a shower and was feeling quite human. It didn't last. Before she'd even unpacked the bags, Mum looked me up and down and, obviously unimpressed, started going on about this woman she'd been chatting to in the dairy aisle. "She was amazing, Polly, four kids, one still a baby, and she was just so groomed and serene." You know, telling it to you it just doesn't sound like much, but it's all the time and, God, it deflates me. I look at her and I think "Why?". She's too smart not to know how it makes me feel.'

Seeing your own upbringing through the prism of motherhood can sometimes make for uncomfortable viewing. Children are born with a keen and unfettered sense of justice. Some days my house rings with cries of, 'It's not fair!', and even when it's irritating, I get it. Life is unfair, and no more so than when you're a child, when you lack the smallest power to do anything about it. So we grow up, suffer the slights of childhood, and shed them when we reach the rational power of adulthood. But how do you process the pain when you discover you were right all along and it really wasn't fair?

> *'One doesn't discover new lands without consenting to lose sight of the shore for a very long time.'*
>
> ANDRÉ GIDE

Motherhood is littered with myths, and it's not only mothers who suffer under their yoke. One of the most pervasive of these myths is that all mothers love all of their children in the same way and to the same degree. Our relationships with our children are as complex and as wildly different as *they* are. Few of us would admit to playing favourites, but it's so tricky not to give in to the child who charms us with a cheeky smile, and equally as difficult not to come down hard when they display the characteristics that drive you nuts. Luckily, for most of us our relationships with each of our children are different enough to rule out a qualitative difference. For some, though, there is the dreadful realisation that they do in fact love one child more than another and that they were loved less than a sibling. For some, like Sue, who get hit with the double whammy, it can literally poison their experience of motherhood.

'I can't remember a time when I didn't realise that my mother loved my sister more than me,' she says. 'It was more than simple favouritism; she and Pip had a connection that essentially excluded me. I used to rationalise it by saying that I was like Dad and Pip was like Mum, so it wasn't surprising that they had a special bond. My parents are so different I still can't work out how they got together in the first place and it wouldn't be an understatement to say that no one was especially surprised when they got divorced. Dad is pretty serious and has a social conscience that can be daunting. Mum's not stupid, but she's just not interested in that side of life, it's all slick and social for her. Growing up with Mum and Pip, I just took refuge in this studious image I'd been given and sort of lived alongside them rather than with them.

'It was only after I became a mum myself, in fact, not until the kids started school, that I started to get really angry with her. I've got three kids and, you know what? They're all different, more different from each other than I am from my husband. I have a really different relationship with each of them, and with one I kind of have to grit my teeth a lot of the time 'cos we just rub each other up the wrong way. But I've done everything I can to make that my responsibility and not their fault. If there's an area where my child and I just don't connect I either find a way to be involved or respect their interests and offer encouragement, then leave them to it. Now I can look back and see that my mother was actually actively cruel. She was punishing me for being like my father and I was excluded in my own home. One of the saddest things is that she made Pip complicit before she was old enough to know what was going on, and now Pip feels this constant guilt. Sometimes I wonder if that's why she decided not to have kids.'

It's not always so big and dramatic, or so negative, but a shift in family dynamics is part of the parcel of parenting. It makes sense for there to be a period of adjustment, for when you go from being a child to a parent, your parents shift up the generational ladder and the change in status is not always easy.

'My father-in-law is your classic patriarch,' says Elspeth. 'He's an incredibly successful man and while he's kind and loving, he's always been very much the head of the family. It wasn't a big deal before kids,

'ONE GENERATION PLANTS
THE TREES; ANOTHER GETS
THE SHADE.'

CONFUCIUS

it was easy just to let him be the boss when we saw him and live our own lives the rest of the time. Once we had kids, it all got a bit messy. 'It was like he found it really hard to come to terms with Brian being a dad; he seemed to be afraid of losing his own power within the family and he suddenly started to undermine Brian whenever he could. It didn't really bother me, in fact, I found it kind of funny, but it started to have a real effect on Brian and then on all of us. The more Brian's dad questioned him, the more Brian questioned himself until he became sort of paralysed, unable to make decisions. It wasn't a problem at home, but it became a big problem at work and things got pretty precarious for a while.

'In the end, I talked Brian into going to see our doctor – it took me about two years to convince him to do it, and it still bothers me that it took so long. The doctor diagnosed depression and referred Brian to a psych. He was freaked out by it, but went along and it was the best thing he could have done. There was no point in trying to change his dad, so he had to change his own reaction to the situation. The funny thing was that once the barbs didn't get to Brian, his dad stopped making them. Looking back, I can see that his dad felt threatened, but I find it harder to respect him now.'

GENERATIONAL STATUS

Whether the members of a family are aware of it or not, status plays a huge role in the dynamics of a family. When children become parents, there's an automatic increase in their generational status and while many parents accept that gracefully, or even gratefully, for others it can be very threatening. You sometimes see it more acutely in families where one parent has been very powerful and as they age their power in the world wanes. He may react by trying to assert greater power within the family arena. It doesn't take a genius to decipher that this grab for power almost always backfires. It goes against the natural order of things. Power and responsibility are meant to cascade down through the generations, and trying to prevent this transfer is a recipe for alienation within the family.

Stepping up to the responsibility plate is one of the defining moments of parenthood. It's a bit like a second chance to cut the apron strings and can be similarly traumatic. While it's easy to appreciate the responsibility entailed in parenthood from a safely academic viewpoint, the reality of assuming it can be slightly overwhelming. I think I gave my mother a few moments of extreme disorientation in the early weeks of baby number one. Not only were her suggestions welcome, I was almost pathetically grateful to have someone more experienced to whom I could defer. Having an acquiescent daughter was a novelty for her, and having a way to delay taking the reins of ultimate reponsibility a relief for me.

MOTHERLESS MOTHERS

Mothering with a role model can have irritating moments, but doing without can be devastating.

'BEING A MOTHERLESS MOTHER WAS SOMETHING I THOUGHT ABOUT A LOT WHILE I WAS PREGNANT. MY MOTHER DIED WHEN I WAS 16 AND I THOUGHT I WAS PREPARING MYSELF FOR WHAT IT WOULD BE LIKE. I COULDN'T HAVE BEGUN TO ANTICIPATE THE RAWNESS OF THE GRIEF THAT CAME FLOODING OVER ME AFTER THE BIRTH. I'M SURE IT WAS INTENSIFIED BY THE BABY BLUES, BUT IT BROUGHT BACK THE SAME KIND OF RAW PAIN I'D FELT WHEN SHE'D DIED. OVER TIME IT GOT EASIER, BUT WHAT SURPRISED ME WERE THE LITTLE THINGS THAT

WOULD SET IT OFF AGAIN. SEEING PHOTOS OF THREE GENERATIONS OF WOMEN WAS ONE OF THE WORST, BUT EVEN HEARING A GIRLFRIEND WHINGE ABOUT HER MUM WOULD SET ME OFF. IN SOME WAYS, MY DAILY LIFE ISN'T THAT DIFFERENT TO A LOT OF MY FRIENDS. PEOPLE MOVE SO MUCH THAT I'D SAY OVER HALF OF MY MUMMY FRIENDS LIVE IN A DIFFERENT CITY TO THEIR PARENTS. THE THING IS, I CAN'T EVEN CALL MY MOTHER. I HAVE SO MANY QUESTIONS I'D LOVE TO ASK HER BUT ALL THERE IS IN ANSWER IS A DEAFENING SILENCE.'

Dealing with young children and the loss of your own mother is an increasingly common problem as women come to motherhood later in life. It doesn't take death to upset the generational balance, estrangement can sometimes be just as final, and so can the realities of ageing parents. Selena has found herself in an increasingly common situation, torn between the needs of her growing children and her ageing parents.

'I didn't have my first child until I was 39,' she says, 'and my parents had my brother and I unusually late in life for their generation. I didn't realise what a burden it would place on me until I was right in the middle of it. As the kids have got older, so have Mum and Dad, and suddenly, they are actually elderly. Mum loves to help out, but it's becoming clearer that she's just not up to it. Physically she can't keep up with them and as she's got older she just gets bewildered by change, she can't cope with situations that wouldn't have phased her in the least a couple of years ago. Dad is even worse, his health is failing and he's so set in his ways he actually finds it difficult to be around the kids for longer than an hour. Sometimes I feel really selfish for moaning about it, they do what they can and really love the kids, but I can't help wishing they were younger. Right now, I'm in a place where I actually need help, but instead of being supported, I'm supporting everybody else.'

While Selena struggles with guilt over her perceived selfishness, she also chafes at the unfairness of carrying the 'daughter load'. 'Occasionally I feel resentment towards my brother,' she says. 'Okay, so he doesn't live nearby, but he's not that far away and yet he basically gets away with doing nothing and practically gets a medal when he deigns to help. But I don't feel any resentment towards Mum and Dad. They spent their lives caring for us, and even when it's hard, I know in my heart I'm just paying them back. I just wish the timing had been better.'

Being noble and forebearing can be a little harder when the parent you're caring for is not your own. Mother-in-law bashing is practically a worldwide sport, but even if your mother-in-law is your bosom buddy, when it comes to shouldering the burden for her care, resentment flares its ugly head. 'I've always adored my mother-in-law,' says Juanita. 'People used to take the mickey, but we were genuinely close. Still, I wasn't prepared for the shock of being expected to take care of her. My husband is an only child, so when his father died, it was only right for him to be there for his mum. Problem is, it hasn't been him being there, it's been me! I love her, but I'm exhausted, and the longer it goes on, the more I resent him for dumping it on me. I know he works, but so do I and we'd already fought the career priority battle when the kids were young, so how come this ended up falling to me?'

I'm unlikely to end up caring for Liza, my mother-in-law, in the same kind of way. For the last few years of her mother's life Liza found herself shouldering the burden of caring for an increasingly sick and elderly woman. Despite living on the other side of the country, while her brother lived around the corner, circumstances dictated that she just get on and do it. The pressure of the situation was unimaginable, she was holding down an extremely high-level job and flying across the country on an almost weekly basis to care for her mother. It was extreme, but not entirely a surprise, when, soon after her mother's death, Liza's body screamed, 'Enough is enough!'. Felled by an aneurism, Liza spent months making a, thankfully, complete recovery and years reassessing her life. One Christmas she sat my husband, his sister and myself down and gave us very clear instructions as to how we were to proceed when she did ultimately end up elderly, ill and dying. It was not an easy session, especially as Liza picked Christmas Eve as being the night on which to do it, but it was a formative and enduring moment in our relationship. By taking me into her confidence and including me while planning for her needs, Liza had offered a level of love and intimacy that made me feel more like a daughter than an in-law. We don't agree on everything, and we wouldn't be human if we didn't irritate the hell out of each other on occasion, but what we do have is a real and loving relationship that has both offered me joy and priceless support. I'm lucky and I know it and, whenever I find myself getting exasperated, I remind myself that things could be very different.

MONSTERS-IN-LAW

'MY MOTHER-IN-LAW WAS SO INTERFERING AND CONTROLLING THAT IT NEARLY BROKE UP OUR MARRIAGE. IT GOT TO THE POINT WHERE I FELT LIKE WE COULDN'T MAKE A DECISION WITHOUT HER APPROVAL, AND SHE WASN'T SHY ABOUT EXERCISING A VETO. I'D GET REALLY ANGRY AT HER AS WELL AS AT MY HUSBAND. IT GOT HARDER AND HARDER TO RESPECT THIS MAN WHEN HE SEEMED TO BE CONSTANTLY GIVING IN TO MUMMY. IN THE END I JUST STARTED WITHDRAWING FROM THE RELATIONSHIP, WHICH WAS PRETTY SCARY. ONE NIGHT I DID A CLASSIC PRINCESS DIANA, YOU KNOW, "THERE ARE THREE PEOPLE IN THIS MARRIAGE", AND THAT FINALLY GOT THROUGH. IT WAS TOUGH FOR HIM TO GET HER TO BACK OFF AND HE FINALLY GOT TO THE POINT WHERE

HE SAID TO HER, "IF YOU MAKE ME CHOOSE BETWEEN YOU AND MY
WIFE, I WILL CHOOSE MY WIFE". THERE WAS A LOT OF PAIN FOR A
LONG TIME, BUT IT WAS WORTH IT. SHE STILL TRIES TO RUN THE SHOW
SOMETIMES, BUT BACKS OFF BEFORE IT GETS TOO MUCH.'

Sometimes it's easier to just toe the line, not rock the boat, keep your
head below the parapet, in fact, protect yourself in any way you can.
When the problem is affecting your children, dealing with it becomes
a matter of necessity. Elizabeth found her mother-in-law difficult
before the relationship was even formalised. 'I fell in love with Jamie
the first night I met him,' she says. 'Sometimes I think that it's a good
thing I love him as much as I do as there's no way I'd want to be
married to his mother otherwise! Ellen's not just a difficult mother-in-
law, she's also a difficult mother, wife and person in general. She can
be a lot of fun, she's a livewire when she wants to be, but she's also
spoilt, pampered, frustrated and controlling. After Sophie was born
things were fantastic. Ellen was totally delighted and just amazing. She
spent heaps of time with us and was brilliant to have around. The first
two years of Sophie's life were some of the best family time we've had.

'Then I got pregnant with Jack. It was weird because Ellen just
seemed completely disinterested and the contrast to the last time was
huge. As soon as Jack was born it got worse; it became really obvious
that I wasn't being paranoid. It wasn't just that Ellen seemed
disinterested in Jack, she seemed to almost not like him and the older
he got, the worse it got. She played favourites and almost seemed to
encourage rivalry between them. It got to the point where I hardly let
Jack spend any time with her as he always came back really
withdrawn. Then we went on a family holiday together. I'm pretty good
with people, and I knew what the problem was with Ellen. She's great
at managing a one-on-one relationship, delightful, in fact, but as soon as

there's a group or family she just has to play games, it's her way of controlling everyone. The holiday was just awful, the kids were fighting, Jamie and I were fighting and Ellen was driving us all nuts.

'Then, one day, she insisted that Jack come into town to go shopping with her. He really didn't want to go, actually clung onto my legs saying, "No". Right in front of him, she told me he was a horrible little boy for not wanting to go with her. Then I snapped. Before I knew it, I'd said, "Of course he doesn't want to go with you, you're nasty to him all the time, why would he want to?" Total shock all round; Ellen actually took a step back and Jamie put his head down ready for the blast. But then she just deflated, took her purse and went off shopping. Jack was amazed, you could almost see him unfurl. It was like Granny had been bullying him and everyone had let her until now; now he felt like Mummy understood and it would all be fine. I wish I'd done it earlier. That's the thing about bullies, they only do it until someone stands up to them.'

Coming to terms with the fact you seem to have landed a monster-in-law can be much more difficult when she's lovely to everyone else yet, for some reason, singles you out for disapprobation. Once it becomes personal it's hard not to take it personally. 'My step-mother-in-law has more than her fair share of hyphens and I reckon it's gone to her head!' jokes India. 'I sometimes feel like she has gone out of her way to make my life as miserable as she can for the whole 12 years I have been with my husband. I was really young when my relationship with Alistair started and pretty emotionally naïve. My sister-in-law, Maddie, became part of the family at the same time as me. Jane was so snide with me and so lovely with Maddie that after a while I started to believe that I was the problem, that I must be a bad person. It seems pathetic now that one person's opinion of me could have such an impact, but I was so shocked by the dislike I encountered that it deeply affected the way I felt about myself.

'Well, 12 years later nothing has changed in terms of the way she treats me, but everything has changed about the way I feel about it. The turning point was so trivial. One weekend we were away in the country on a family holiday and I was swinging between hurt and simmering fury about the constant digs. Then, after lunch, I took my plate to the sink, rinsed it and put it in the dishwasher. Jane, using her most condescending voice, said, "Oh for goodness sake, India, are you not aware there is a drought on?". I apologised and, cheeks burning, started clearing away the mess on the counter. Then Maddie walked in, rinsed her plate and put it in the dishwasher. "Oh Maddie," cooed Jane, "you are such a sweet and helpful girl." For the first time I could see how totally absurd the whole thing was and just burst out laughing. Now when Jane tries to lord it over me I just look at her with a vague expression on my face and say, "Hmmm? What? Oh yes, right, whatever …" and drift away. It drives her nuts and never fails to make me feel better.'

'I ADORE MY MOTHER-IN-LAW; SHE'S A CLASSIC GREEK MAMA AND LIVES FOR HER CHILDREN AND GRANDCHILDREN. SHE HAS A HEART OF GOLD AND PAMPERS ME LIKE YOU WOULDN'T BELIEVE. SHE BRINGS OVER FOOD, CLEANS OUR HOUSE CONSTANTLY AND IS ALWAYS WHISKING THE KIDS AWAY SO THAT STAMOS AND I CAN BE ALONE TOGETHER. I SUSPECT THAT SHE DOES THAT TO GIVE US TIME TO MAKE MORE BABIES; THREE'S NOT ENOUGH FOR HER, THOUGH IT'S PLENTY FOR US!'

They say you can choose you friends but not your family. Marriage may no longer be for life, but once you've bred, in-laws tend to stick around regardless. Techniques for dealing with them range from the sanguine to the absurd. 'I hate my in-laws,' confesses Tessa, 'and frankly the feeling's pretty mutual. We disagree on essentially everything and they are convinced that working makes me a negligent mother. But, you know what, I just don't care. You see, they adore my children and are the most loving and indulgent grandparents imaginable. When I see them together I just think, "Who cares what they think of me?" and get on with living my own life.'

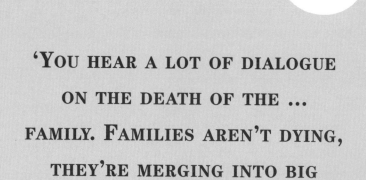

'YOU HEAR A LOT OF DIALOGUE
ON THE DEATH OF THE ...
FAMILY. FAMILIES AREN'T DYING,
THEY'RE MERGING INTO BIG
CONGLOMERATES.'

ERMA BOMBECK

In the mix

'If you cannot get rid of the family skeleton, you may as well make it dance.'

GEORGE BERNARD SHAW

I hate the term 'blended families', it always makes me think of those terrible penguin jokes (You know, what's black and white and red all over? A penguin in a blender ...), but I'm yet to come across a better phrase. It's hard to sum up all the special dynamics, needs and dilemmas of any family, let alone one that has been rebuilt without a manual. Step-parents get a fairly rough rap in fiction, popular imagination and statistical surveys. It must be hard enough to take on a job as immense as helping to bring up someone else's children without feeling like public enemy number one.

All parents will, at some stage, feel as though their child hates them. It's hard to believe that the adorable toddler who, frankly, seems to think you are a deity, movie star and magician in one pretty gorgeous package could ever be less than admiring, but one day, they will see that you also have feet of clay and once they've recovered from the shock their reaction can be fairly testing. 'I hate you, Mum!', 'I wish I'd never been born!' and 'I never asked to be born into this family!' were just some of the choice (and printable) phrases I threw at my parents as I battled the storm of adolescence. At the very least they could reassure themselves that deep down I still did love them and that no matter what I said, they would always be my parents (hmmm, not such a good deal, really, when I think about it). But what if you are not bound to the child by the indissoluble ties of blood? What if the core of your love burns for the child's parent, not purely for them? How do you referee the inevitable skirmishes between your precious child and your partner? And, are you still a mother to a child you've grown to love after you've separated from her father?

FAMILIES

There are some amazing family structures living and evolving in the real world. You read about them, see them on television, hear the usual suspects pontificate about them, but until you live it, it can be hard to appreciate just how sprawling the definition of 'family' can be. What is especially amazing, and hopeful, to me is the extent to which children seem to take these multilayered structures in their stride. A family set-up that sounds outlandish on paper can appear completely natural to children. I was driving my son and his friend home from an after-school class and they were chatting away about nothing more exciting than laser swords. A minute dissection of the merits of various laser swords led on to the movies they'd seen and the circumstances in which they'd seen them. Tom was chatting away about his cousins, and his buddy was talking about his brothers and sisters. As a prurient and pedantic adult, I know full well that their conversation should have been littered with the word 'step' but for these little boys the bonds of marriage and remarriage were as strong and natural as those of blood. They weren't interested in explaining to each other which of those siblings or cousins was a full-blooded one, which was a half and which was entirely a 'step'. To them, it simply didn't matter. What did matter was the quality of the relationship, the amount of love they felt for the other little people who made up their families.

No one would deny that the break-up of a marriage is difficult emotional territory. Whether that marriage is torn apart through death, disaster and divorce or the relationship simply drifts apart and disintegrates, there are ramifications for all the members of that family: parents, children and grandchildren, not to mention siblings, aunts, cousins etc. Rarely is the dissolution of a marriage undertaken lightly and I have never personally witnessed a marriage breakdown where both parents were not fully committed to making each step of the journey as gentle as possible for the children involved. There are excellent programs and books devoted to the process of helping children through divorce and the death of a parent. I am categorically not an expert in this area and am unable to offer appropriate advice. What I have tried to do in this chapter is to paint a picture of what happens next. To start from the point where the breakdown has already taken place, and explore the different ways in which families put themselves back together.

'WE LIVE IN A FAIRLY LAIDBACK PART OF TOWN AND MY TWO GIRLS GO TO THE LOCAL PRIMARY SCHOOL. ONE OF DAPHNE'S BEST FRIENDS HAS TWO MOTHERS, A LESBIAN COUPLE WHO HAD HER VIA IVF. I'M PRETTY OPEN-MINDED, BUT I GUESS I WAS STILL TAKEN ABACK WHEN I WORKED THAT ONE OUT FOR THE FIRST TIME. THE GIRLS PUT ME TO

SHAME, THEY ARE ALL SO NONCHALANT ABOUT IT. WHEN DAPHNE INTRODUCES EMILY TO PEOPLE FOR THE FIRST TIME SHE'LL ALWAYS SAY, "THIS IS EMILY, SHE HAS TWO MUMMIES", AND AS FAR AS THEY ARE CONCERNED, THAT'S THE END OF THE MATTER.'

Take your average primary school and you will find children from intact families, those who live with both parents equally, some who have weekday and weekend arrangements. There are some who have lost a parent to death or estrangement, some who were born to women who knew they would be single from day one. A couple of children live with their grandparents and there is at least one who lives with her stepfather despite the fact that he and her mother are divorced. The thing is, none of these children comes with a label that lays it all bare. Their home circumstances are something you learn about as you come to know them, and often turn out to be the least interesting thing about them. The struggles and battles that go into building the edifice of the family usually take place far from the eyes and ears of the children who live within them.

Imogen admits that her family is unusual by any standards. 'We're like the anti-Brady Bunch,' she says. 'Colin and I have six children and four marriages between us. His children come in matching pairs of two, neither of my children have the same father, and between us we have none. But his children are mine and vice versa.' Imogen makes it very clear that taking each other's children on board has been an important part of creating a family from very disparate parts. 'It's been incredibly hard and I think it's been harder for me than anyone. Colin's kids were pretty much all grown up when we got together. He hadn't been there for them when they were little and he decided that he wanted to do everything he could to make that up to them. So we got an enormous house, gathered the kids from all over the place and tried to be a "family". I was willing to give it a go despite my misgivings, but it ended up being a complete disaster. After two years of being the wicked stepmother, I decided I'd had enough. I'm not the type to yell, scream or threaten, so I just said to Colin, "I can't live like this, so I guess I'm going to have to leave." I did leave, but Colin came with me, and now we live together with my youngest. We still make up a family, a slightly strange one, but a family. I'm glad we tried it, it meant so much to Colin, but I think I knew from the beginning that you can't force a family into shape, you have to let it grow.'

The one thing that Imogen has insisted on is that every year, once a year, no matter what everyone is doing and no matter where they are, everybody gathers to celebrate Colin's birthday. 'Colin, his daughter, one of his sons and my daughter all have their birthday in the same month. No matter what else is going on we get together and have a proper party. All grievances and problems are left at the door and on that one day we celebrate each other and the fact that we are a family.'

Love is not solely the province of the young, nor of the firm and beautiful. While there's no denying that Cinderella lucked out when it came to her stepmother, in reality, love and romance are not reserved for her and her prince. As for happily ever after, well that's just a cop-out of an ending. Even as a child I suspected that the really interesting stuff happened after the story ended and that there was no way it was all happy. There's no denying that the fairy stories we are told as children leave an indelible imprint. Somewhere deep inside, we are all Cinderella, feeling safe in the belief that one day our prince will come. When he does, it's unlikely that either of us will look the part, but it doesn't mean we won't feel it. Love is a mystery and there are no guarantees that when it arrives it will come in a conventional package. Love accessorised with wrinkles and kids is deep and vital nonetheless. Baggage doesn't undo passion, but it can make it harder to negotiate.

'I WAS REALLY QUITE SMITTEN WITH JOHN BEFORE I FOUND OUT MUCH ABOUT HIM. IN FACT, I'D BEEN WATCHING HIM FROM ACROSS THE OFFICE FOR ABOUT A YEAR BEFORE ANYTHING HAPPENED. WHEN I FOUND OUT HE WAS DIVORCED WITH CHILDREN IT WAS A SURPRISE, BUT IT DIDN'T PUT ME OFF. THE FACT THAT HE HAD JOINT CUSTODY MADE ME FALL MORE IN LOVE WITH HIM, AND IT WAS ALREADY PRETTY DEEP. IT GAVE HIM OTHER DIMENSIONS; IN THIS PARTICULAR ERA, MANY MEN MAKE THE MONEY BUT DON'T TAKE ON THE SAME CHILDCARE BURDEN, BUT HERE, HE WAS SAYING, "MY KIDS ARE SO IMPORTANT TO ME THAT I'LL SACRIFICE SOME OF MY INCOME AND FREEDOM TO MAKE SURE MY CHILDREN HAVE EQUAL ACCESS TO ME".'

Dating can be a scary and dangerous game and when your preferred partner comes with a ready-made team, it can make for a crowded field. That is not necessarily a bad thing, but it does mean it's difficult to be casual about aspects of the relationship most people take for granted.

Michelle had known Sergio socially for years before they became a couple. 'We'd been on the edge of the same crowd at university,' says Michelle, 'and although we weren't especially close, we ended up working in the same field so we'd run into each other once in a while. Sergio and Alison were married for eight years and had two boys. We didn't start seeing each other until years after his divorce and knowing his history meant that, for me, his family was an automatic part of him. We got together at a conference in Canberra, and that night was the only night I got to sleep over without thinking about it first. We knew straightaway that this was going to be a serious relationship and that we needed to take his children into account from day one. It's funny to think that I was at both of his weddings, once as a plus-one and the second time as his bride.'

It's easy to feel that being a father adds a special something to a man's allure even while having children may detract from a woman's. All my husband had to do to get half of the old women in the neighbourhood swooning was strap a baby into the pram and hit the park. He'd hardly be able to make it from one end to the other without being mobbed by approving grannies. 'You're so good,' they'd coo, 'taking your children to the park.' He'd come home and taunt me with the lavish praised he'd received that day. The only comments I ever got were along the lines of, 'Are you sure he's warm enough, dear?'. Putting jealousy aside, it's easy to see how a man's commitment to his children can enhance his appeal in the eyes of his partner. If ever my husband wants to fan the spark of romance, he's guaranteed a good chance simply by shouldering an extra proportion of the domestic burden.

For a woman still sizing up the qualities of a potential partner, watching the way in which he cares for his children can be immensely appealing. 'Watching him run a bath for his kids was a real turning point for me,' remembers Diana. 'It's such a simple domestic act, something that has to be done every day, but watching him actively caring for Jess and Lulu made me feel that I'd be able to trust him to care for me.'

The first flush of infatuation is a heady but brief time in the history of any relationship and the enforced domesticity of an instant family can hurry the process on its way. With the move towards shared custody after a divorce, the pace of a new romance can become dictated by the routines of family life very quickly. There is added impetus to take things slowly when children are involved; few responsible parents would be comfortable with introducing a stream of new partners into their children's lives. Once the line between dating and mating is crossed, going back is not easy and there is a lot of adjusting to be done by all involved.

Meeting the kids can be scarier than meeting the in-laws, but it's not always a nightmare. 'I had fallen in love with this man who obviously had a real commitment to his kids and I prized that,' says Pia. 'Once we declared our feelings and intentions, I was really concerned about how the girls would feel about me, how they'd react to me. He'd had a girlfriend between his ex-wife and going out with me, so the girls already had the experience of Dad having a new woman. I assumed they'd have some negative feelings towards me; society makes it clear that kids from a broken marriage are going to be resentful of a new stepmum. I was expecting some kind of a difficult situation and I was prepared to make the transition as easy as it needed to be for them. I was aware of it, of making sure they came first and showing them that I understood they would need time to accept me. The first time I met the girls, they invited me over for dinner; I'm sure Steve suggested it, but they issued the invitation. I came over for spag bol, there was no pressure or atmosphere of sizing up; it was completely relaxed and everyone was at ease with each other. It's been like that ever since.'

Pia counts herself lucky that her introduction to family life with Steve was so smooth and credits him for handling it with grace and foresight. 'He was madly in love with me and desperate for it to work,' she says. He knew if we were going to work as a couple then we'd need to find a way to work as a family. I think he handled it really well, but I also think it was partly just about personality. The girls and I just fit together really well.'

OTHER PEOPLE'S CHILDREN

Love conquering all is an image that is deeply entrenched in our society, but there are some challenges that can make that smooth path really rocky, and a difficult relationship with each other's children is one of them. 'Taking on each other's children has been a really complex operation,' says Jenny. 'Between us we've got five, so as a family we're dealing with seven really different personalities, plus ex-wives and husbands, and there can be serious fireworks. I don't think it's just about his children versus mine. The fireworks are just as likely to be between parent and child, or the kids themselves. I find one of his sons just too difficult to deal with. He makes no effort to look after himself and acts like a child despite being an adult. In the end we just had to agree to keep a certain amount of distance between us. On the other hand, I feel that Alan is really distant with my daughter when she'd really like him to be close. There's a feeling in the family that him being close to Alicia would be a betrayal of his relationship with his own daughter. It's tough stuff trying to manage everybody; the thing that keeps us together is how deeply we love each other. We were meant to be together and finding each other later in life just means we have a bit more to deal with than most.'

Emotional quandaries are not the only issues that demand attention. Taking responsibility for a partner's children also involves many practical alterations. Anne was single, successful and fancy-free when she met John. 'I spent a lot of time preparing for the emotional fallout that I assumed would be part and parcel of us getting together. We took the whole thing really slowly and made sure that the kids had adjusted to the idea of "us" before we started living together. What I forgot to do was make sure that *I* was fully adjusted to it. Now I realise how naïve I was to think that the only impact it would have on my life would be emotional. It took a long time to get used to being an instant mum. I was used to being able to do whatever I wanted – go to the gym, out for coffee, catch an exhibition – and suddenly, I was doing the school run and watching football matches, with basically no time for my own life. I don't resent it, I just didn't expect it, but I guess it's just the tensions of family life. Sometimes I think that at least if I'd given birth to them I would have got the flowers and announcements first, instead of going straight to a routine of dentists and dance classes.'

Responsibility can be a double-edged sword when the children you're caring for are not your own. Taking responsibility for a child inevitably involves making decisions on their behalf. We don't always get it right, but we do our best, and even when we're unsure which way to go, at least we know we have the authority to go ahead. The lines of authority can become very blurred when the child is not your own. There can be few who have tackled the task without having the classic, 'You're not my mother!' thrown in their face. It can be even worse when the father sides with the child.

On the flipside, allowing your new partner to exert authority within the house can be a painful experience. 'Davey and Phil get on really well,' explains Mary, 'except when it comes to rules. I've been with Phil since Dave was two and they've always really loved each other. I share custody with my ex-husband and we do the best job that we can. We get on pretty well and agree on the big decisions, but we live our day-to-day lives really differently. It was one of the reasons we broke up; I need my life to be organised and efficient, it's the only way I feel comfortable. I had a chaotic childhood and never really felt safe so it's important to me to give my son a stable homelife. We have set times for meals, waking, homework, sleeping and things like TV and computer games. Alan, my ex, is the complete opposite; basically Davey can do what he likes when he likes at Dad's. The first two days of every week have become harder and harder as Davey has got older. He loves the freedom he has with his dad and resents having to do things my way when he gets home. What makes it worse is when Phil gets involved in enforcing the routine. Dave gets wild when Phil tells him what to do and sometimes I feel really caught in the middle. Part of me just wants to shut Phil out of the discussion and keep it between me and Davey, but the reality is that this is Phil's home too, and he has to be allowed to set limits.'

'JAMIE AND I HAD TO FIND A BALANCE WITH THE GIRLS THAT GAVE ME ROOM TO BE THE BOSS, TOO. IT'S NOT THAT I WANT TO BE HEAVY WITH THEM, BUT EVERY SECOND WEEK THEY ARE LIVING IN MY HOUSE. I'M COOKING FOR THEM, RUNNING THEM AROUND, LOVING THEM AND I NEED TO BE ABLE TO RUN THE SHOW LIKE ANY OTHER MOTHER WOULD. WHEN WE GOT TOGETHER I EMBRACED HIS CHILDREN WHOLE-HEARTEDLY, INCLUDING THE EXTRA RESPONSIBILITY, AND, IN RETURN, THEY NEEDED TO LEARN TO RESPECT ME AS WELL. IT'S THE ONLY WAY TO OPERATE LIKE A NORMAL FAMILY.'

LIVING WITH THE EX

Picking a partner with a ready-made family also involves learning to live with the ex. Degrees of contact will vary, but the children's mother will inevitably continue to play a role in the family you are busy building. 'Lena reacted strongly when Alex and I got together,' says Vivien. 'I suppose it's not really surprising, but I'd assumed that, since she'd left him, it wouldn't bother her when he found someone else. There were some pretty big battles to start with. Until I came along, she'd pretty much stayed away from Alex's house, then suddenly, she kept finding reasons to be there. I figured the only way to handle it was to give everyone time to settle in and just see what happened. The tension finally erupted over what the kids were going to call me. Ollie was only four when Alex and I started living together and he wanted to call me Mum. We explained that was Leda's special name and we'd need to find another one for me. Then Mia, who was 14, suggested "S'mum", an abbreviation of stepmum. Everyone was happy with that and Jeremy, who was eight, thought it was especially cool as it could also stand for "special mum". Leda went ballistic when she heard that, told the kids they couldn't call me that, she was their mum and the special one. I can understand it must have been painful for her, but I thought the way she handled it, banning the kids from using it, was pretty harsh.'

Dysfunctional relationships are not an inevitable part of blended families. There are plenty of mixed-up 'normal' families and lots of created families that operate beautifully, if uniquely. Rita met her husband, Jack, while he was still married to Beth. 'We met at a dance party and it was love at first sight,' she explains. 'As soon as I realised he was married, that was it, I headed off and put him out of my head. Two years later, we bumped into each other. By then, he and Beth had separated and straightaway it was all on. We were married within a year and were madly in love. It was pretty hard for me, getting used to his boys; I'd had nothing to do with kids and was out of my depth. We'd talked about having children together, but he'd made it clear he didn't want any more. It was the only thing that had made me think twice about marrying him, but I was so in love I couldn't walk away. In the end we managed to get pregnant the same week we got married! It's been a rough ride, but we've really managed to make it work. Believe it or not, staying close to Beth has been one of the keys to getting it right. We're an incredibly modern family. Her new partner goes kite surfing with Jack. When I came out of hospital the first night after having Ellie, we had the boys 'cos it was our week and we never change the weeks, so she came round to cook our dinner to give us a break. She's cooking dinner in our kitchen, going, "Oh, you've put things in a different place to when I lived here." We all live near each other and share the kids, including my daughter. The other day I was pushing Ellie in the pram to get the boys from school. I have to walk past Beth's shop to get there, we had a chat and she suggested I leave Ellie with her. So I did. She looked after my daughter while I picked her sons up from school. It sounds crazy, but somehow it just works.'

'ONE OF THE BEAUTIFUL THINGS ABOUT BEING A STEPMOTHER IS THAT I CAN CARE FOR KATE AND MILES LIKE THEY ARE MY OWN, BUT STILL OFFER SOMETHING DIFFERENT. KATE'S A TEENAGER NOW, AND I'VE BECOME THE PERSON SHE CAN TALK TO ABOUT ALL THOSE THINGS THAT AN ADOLESCENT JUST CAN'T SAY TO THEIR MUM AND DAD. OUR DAUGHTER, OLIVIA, IS ONLY SIX MONTHS OLD, BUT I HOPE ONE DAY SHE HAS SOMEONE SHE CAN TURN TO LIKE KATIE TURNS TO ME. IN FACT, I WISH I'D HAD THAT WHEN I WAS HER AGE.'

Forming bonds with older children is a very different beast to falling in love with a baby. We're often told that the most important bonding period is at the very beginning; this may be true, but it doesn't exclude the possibility of forming lifelong bonds with your partner's children. Your relationship with them is bound to ebb and flow, just as it would with your own children, yet over time, tolerance and acceptance can grow into fondness and then genuine love. 'They're part of his life, they come as a package,' says Pamela. 'I don't know any other way, but I also love them independently for who they are. I've sometimes thought, what happens if the relationship doesn't work? I'm so committed to them I can't imagine life without them. I'd never be able to withdraw from them.'

When a couple comes together bringing children with them, the decision to have a child can cement the union, but it can also be threatening for existing children. 'When Mike and I told the kids we were getting married, they all seemed to take it well except for his daughter, Daisy, who was 13. She went really quiet, so I asked her if she was okay. She said, 'I don't mind if you get married so long as you don't have a baby'. I took a deep breath and said that might happen, it might not, but we can't promise that. We haven't had a child yet and it's still an issue for her now.'

Jasmine comes at this picture from the other end. 'When I was 13, my mother remarried, then, when I was 14, she and Chris, my stepfather, told me they were having a baby. I was completely horrified. More than anything, I was just so embarrassed, because if they were having a baby, they must have been having sex, and that was something I just didn't want to think about. At that age I'd probably have been happiest if they'd slept in twin beds; getting pregnant just seemed like they were flaunting it. All I could think was "ick".'

Russian author Leo Tolstoy wrote, 'Happy families are all alike; but each unhappy family is unhappy in its own way'. I disagree, no two families are the same. Happy or not, normal or not, families are at heart a collection of individuals and the prevailing dynamic can only be unique. Whether you get it right or wrong has nothing to do with how you put it together in the first place. Putting together a blended family may entail a greater degree of difficulty, but as with every 'normal' family the result depends on luck, hard work and a whole lot of love.

'TO NOURISH CHILDREN AND
RAISE THEM AGAINST THE ODDS
IS AT ANY TIME, IN ANY PLACE,
MORE VALUABLE THAN TO FIX
BOLTS IN CARS OR DESIGN
NUCLEAR WEAPONS.'

MARILYN FRENCH

'WOMEN AND CATS WILL DO AS
THEY PLEASE AND MEN AND
DOGS SHOULD RELAX AND GET
USED TO THE IDEA.'

ROBERT A. HEINLEIN

Boys and girls

'If you want anything said, ask a man. If you want something done, ask a woman.'

Margaret Thatcher

I came into this business of mothering firmly convinced that human characteristics were all about nurture. I thought that each person on this earth was born with a clean slate and who they would become was defined by their experience of life. So when my son was one I bought him a baby doll; he was delighted with it, delighted to have something to swing around his head and kick down the hall. The doll then sat neglected until my second son discovered it and proceeded to draw on its face and pull out its hair. Stuffed toys fared no better in our household; the enormous pile of gorgeous teddies given to the boys by loving grandparents and friends was either ignored or used to build a platform from which to scale forbidden heights. Then came my daughter and, with no obvious encouragement, she collected all the poor refugee dolls and teddies and gathered them to her. She talked to them, took them to the toilet and restored them to life. Suddenly, I wasn't so sure where I stood in the great gender debate, and just as suddenly I realised that it couldn't be less important. What I had miraculously done was give birth to three little people, and if they chose to behave like stereotypes, more power to them.

'THE MORE KIDS YOU HAVE THE LESS IT MATTERS WHETHER THEY ARE BOYS OR GIRLS. ONE OF MY GIRLFRIENDS HAD HER FIRST BABY, A LITTLE BOY, AND OVER THE COURSE OF THE FIRST FEW MONTHS I FINALLY GOT AROUND TO CATCHING UP WITH HER. AS WELL AS TAKING A COUPLE OF PRESENTS, I TOOK SOME CLOTHES THAT MY SON HAD GROWN OUT OF. THEY'VE GOT SO MANY GORGEOUS CLOTHES WHEN THEY'RE REALLY LITTLE AND THEY GROW OUT OF THEM BEFORE THEY HAVE A CHANCE TO RUIN THEM. SO I TAKE THIS BAG ROUND AND I'M PULLING STUFF OUT AND GETTING ALL NOSTALGIC WHEN SHE KIND OF GIVES ME THIS LOOK AND SAYS, "WHAT ARE THESE?".

'I SAY, "THEY'RE PYJAMAS, LILY, YOU KNOW, KIDS SLEEP IN THEM?" TURNS OUT THE PROBLEM IS THAT THEY'RE PINK. LILY IS SURE THAT I'VE BROUGHT SOME OF POPPY'S CLOTHES BY ACCIDENT. FUNNY THING IS, THEY WERE FREDDIE'S JIM-JAMS AND I NEVER THOUGHT THERE WAS ANYTHING WEIRD ABOUT PUTTING A BOY IN PINK ELEPHANT PYJAMAS. I GUESS THAT'S JUST THE DIFFERENCE BETWEEN BABY ONE AND BABY THREE.'

THE GENDER DEBATE

Take the time to visit your local playing fields any Saturday in winter and it's pretty obvious that, to a certain extent, the great gender debate has ironed itself out. Soccer has been a great leveller with boys and girls playing alongside each other, especially in the lower grades. Parents are busy whisking their sons and daughters to yoga, art and tae kwon do regardless of their gender.

Problem is, the message doesn't seem to have trickled down through the ranks. My second son has a little saying, for him it's almost like a mantra. It goes like this, 'Girls are smarter than boys and boys are stronger than girls'. No amount of rationalisation will convince him that the truth may be slightly more complicated than that, even being beaten up by his little sister failed to shake his conviction. He's only four and is bound to grow out of it, but I can't help feeling that the message will resonate somewhere deep in his psyche.

At least he's being fashionable; his preschool truism reflects the current debate that seems to boil down to 'the problem with boys'. When I was a kid, the problem with boys was that they hogged the maths prizes and always won kiss-chasey; which of those worried you more depended entirely on what kind of girl you were, and I'm not telling! I grew up during the innocent 70s, in the early flush of widespread feminism when girls could do whatever they wanted, and so could boys, but then, what was new? The push to liberate girls from their supposed destiny as nothing more than the bearers of the next generation is, of course, not a product of the 70s.

The fight for women's liberation began as far back as the 18th century, and possibly even earlier: Mary Wollstonecraft's *A Vindication of the Rights of Women* was published in 1792; Emily Wilding Davison threw herself in front of the King's horse at the 1913 Derby crying, 'Votes for women!'; WWII saw boys sent to the front and women 'manning' the factory floor. Popular history has it that the return to the home front was facilitated by the mass consumption of sedatives, the wonder drug of the 50s. Bras were burned, treatises written and a generation of women took great joy in telling their daughters they could be anything they wanted to be. So what happened? How is that so many of those girls have ended up, as women, feeling cheated and lied to? And when did the emancipation of girls mutate into 'the problem with boys'?

I graduated from high school with the misguided notion that I could be and do anything I wanted. It's a marvellous notion and it's not hard to see the thinking that lay underneath it: tell children, especially girls, that they can do everything and then just sit back and watch them do it. It was such a hopeful time; corporate corridors thronged with shoulder pads and superwoman was bursting out of her chrysalis to take on the world. I think most of my Year 12 class genuinely believed that a future of unlimited achievement lay ahead of us. We wouldn't just break the glass ceiling, it would shatter under the force of our momentum. Babies would come, not that we thought much about them, but for most of us, their future presence was indistinct yet given. It made such a pretty picture and photographed fabulously; we'd be just like the women in magazines who strode home from their stimulating jobs to their immaculate homes to pass the evening with their gorgeous partners and divine children. Unfortunately, we were too callow to realise that just as that photo shoot required an army of staff, so would the lives we envisaged. I seriously doubt that this airbrushed image was much in the minds of the women who fought so hard to set us free, but for many of us it left a lasting, and divisive, inheritance.

I REFUSE TO TELL MY CHILDREN THEY CAN DO AND BE ANYTHING THEY WANT. I TELL THEM THAT IF THEY SET THEIR MINDS TO ACHIEVING SOMETHING AND WORK HARD AT IT, THE CHANCES ARE THEY WILL SUCCEED. ANYTHING ELSE IS JUST A LIE AS FAR AS I'M CONCERNED. SOMEWHERE ALONG THE LINE THE MESSAGE GOT CONFUSED. LIKE A

GENERATIONAL GAME OF CHINESE WHISPERS, IT WENT FROM BEING 'YOU CAN BE ANYTHING' TO 'YOU CAN BE EVERYTHING' AND ALONG THE WAY, 'YOU CAN HAVE IT ALL' TURNED INTO 'SO LONG AS YOU DO IT ALL'. HOW DID IT HAPPEN THAT WE ALL CONSPIRED TO SET THE BAR SO HIGH THAT A LINGERING FEELING OF FAILURE BECAME A GENERATIONAL MALAISE?

For a start, there's no sense in pointing the finger of blame at the women who came before us. In fact, there's nothing to be gained by trying to blame anyone; we are doing what our forebears did, taking our historical legacy and trying to drive it forward in the best way we can. It's terribly fashionable right now to blame feminism for the work/life/balance confronting so many women, mothers or otherwise. Feminism was, and is, simply a movement, hard fought and won, to liberate women from the shackles that bind them. Before you move right along, it's important to remember that we once were merely chattels, the property of our fathers and then our husbands. Our futures were easy to plan as our options were limited to, and defined by, our relationships – mother, sister, daughter, wife. What feminism has done is give us the right to make choices for ourselves; it cannot provide solutions for every conundrum, but we can keep on trying and fighting to make things better.

Which is often when we find ourselves back in the classroom. School is an undoubtedly formative time in any child's life; it's also the place where gender first rears its ugly head. Why is it that children, who have happily played, slept and even bathed alongside each other regardless of the shape of their genitalia, suddenly and mysteriously align themselves along gender lines in the first few years of primary school? 'Girls rock and boys suck' is the considered explanation of my neighbour's daughter. 'But why?' I ask, and receive in reply a look so withering that no elaboration is required. Education has gone from being something reserved solely for boys to a mandatory rite of passage for all children. Numeracy, literacy and citizenship may be all the rage with those setting the curriculum, but for many children school is an essentially tribal experience and when warfare erupts it is often the boys versus the girls.

When conducting social experiments on a massive scale, it makes sense to go to your audience. And where do you find a captive audience of supposedly malleable littlies? At school. And what do you do if you are a socially responsible nation? You educate your children in both academia and contemporary mores and, if you take it seriously, you continually improve both the substance and methods of your education system. So why is there a common perception that schools have swung from discriminating against girls to discriminating against boys?

'I HATE PARENT-TEACHER INTERVIEWS, EVEN MORE NOW THAT I'M A PARENT. LIAM DOES WELL ENOUGH IN TERMS OF PROGRESS AND MARKS – IN FACT, I'M ALWAYS IMPRESSED AT WHAT HE CAN DO. MAYBE I'M JUST GETTING OLD, BUT HIS LESSONS SEEM A LOT MORE COMPLICATED THAN THEY WERE WHEN I WAS A KID. WHAT I HATE IS THAT EVERY TERM WE END UP SKIPPING THROUGH THE WORKSHEETS SO THAT THE TEACHER CAN GET DOWN TO THE PROBLEMS WITH LIAM'S BEHAVIOUR. I DON'T THINK HE'S AN ANGEL, I KNOW HE'S NOT, BUT I FIND THESE INTERVIEWS INCREDIBLY FRUSTRATING BECAUSE THE THINGS I'M EXPECTED TO HELP HIM GROW OUT OF STRIKE ME AS JUST THE CHARACTERISTICS OF LITTLE BOYS. HE'S TOO COMPETITIVE, FIDGETS TOO MUCH, TALKS TOO LOUDLY AND HAS A "SHORT ATTENTION SPAN". I UNDERSTAND THAT THESE THINGS ARE DISRUPTIVE IN THE CLASSROOM AND THAT IT'S UP TO US TO HELP MODIFY HIS BEHAVIOUR, WHAT I DON'T UNDERSTAND IS WHEN AND WHY THESE QUALITIES WENT FROM BEING NORMAL TO BEING BAD.'

ARE GIRLS 'THE SAFER OPTION'?

Ask any woman pregnant with her first child whether she wants a boy or a girl and the chances are she'll say 'I really don't mind, just so long as it's healthy'. Push a little harder and it's remarkable to discover how many of those women are secretly hankering for a baby girl. It used to be that boys were the prized delivery; smart women produced the heir, then the spare and finally a frivolous girl to keep her company. In some parts of the world, little has changed and there is international debate at the highest level about ultrasound tests being used for selective termination. And male babies are strongly desired. So, why is it that here in the affluent West, girls are the unspoken desire of so many women?

My boy's little mantra, 'smart versus strong', is really just a crude distillation of the received wisdom that girls are manageable infants, good at school and altogether less trouble to raise than boys.

While government researchers calculate to the last dollar the amount of money required to raise a child and society debates the 'cost' to women of having children it's easy to begin seeing them as an investment. The trouble is, that by definition, an investment is supposed to bring a return and, for some reason, girls are often seen as the safer option. From where I stand, children are no more an 'investment' than they are a 'sacrifice'; they are people and each one of them as different as can be.

> *'The basic discovery about any people is the discovery of the relationship between its men and its women.'*
>
> PEARL S. BUCK

It's easy to exaggerate gender differences, but it's hard to deny that most boys seem to display a greater concentration of certain characteristics, and most girls other ones altogether (have I qualified that one enough for you?). Okay, I'll be bolder, children are, as we've established throughout this book, unique individuals in their own right. However, and this is a big one for me, if we are prepared to bitch about our husbands, boyfriends, brothers and fathers for behaving like men, how can we deny that our sons are, in fact, boys and our daughters, girls? How many times have you, or a girlfriend, had a whinge that revolved around your significant other and ended with one party asserting 'typical bloody man'?

So I'm going to go out on a limb and tentatively assert that it is vaguely possible there are some characteristics that could be thought to be more prevalent among one gender than another. Clear enough for you? Okay, maybe it's alright to say that sometimes boys will be boys and girls will be girls. While I may seem to be ambivalent on this subject, I find it incredibly difficult even to entertain the possibility of boys and girls, men and women, being broadly different from each other. It's such an article of faith for my generation that if men and women are equal, which they assuredly are, then they must therefore be the same. Problem is, that as a mother, I am regularly confronted by the apparent differences between boys and girls. Whether those differences are the result of nature or nurture has been debated by infinitely better qualified, and educated, minds than mine.

I entered motherhood standing firmly in the nurture line and then commenced to queue-hop furiously, one day, nature, the next, nurture. Maybe both, possibly neither, but more importantly, from a practical point of view, does it really matter? Science and ideology are equally unwieldy tools and clearly not designed with my daily routine in mind. Experience has taught me it is better to acknowledge my own ignorance and instead, choose to go with instinct. And my instinct is that we'd be far better off learning to truly understand the complex equations we ignored in long-ago maths classes whereby things can be equivalent, different but essentially equal.

Never underestimate the sweetness of a boy's love for his mother. You are their first 'everywoman' and that kind of adoration is hard to come by, so enjoy it while it lasts. Let your daughter be Daddy's little princess if that's what works for her, and appreciate the infinitely more satisfying role of showing her who she can be simply by being you.

ARE GIRLS AND BOYS DIFFERENT?

Talking about offering ill-informed opinions, I decided that this was one subject that deserved the input of the truly experienced. I waylaid three teachers, all of whom come equipped with several decades teaching experience yet remain fresh and open-minded (they know who they are and I do prefer to remain in their good books!). I asked each of them the same question, 'Do you think that boys and girls are different?'. Not one of them hesitated before answering. The general consensus was a resounding yes. They offered the standard warnings and provisos in regard to individuality and the dangers of overdoing generalisation, but essentially, there was a very strong feeling that boys and girls are different.

The principal offered an observation that made Will's mantra a little less far-fetched. 'In terms of learning and teaching techniques there is an observable difference in the way that boys and girls respond. Research has shown that boys tend to have a much greater need for physical movement and this needs to be taken into account as it can have a measurable affect on their ability to concentrate. It's also been shown that boys generally respond better when the learning program is more directed and has distinct goals. The interesting thing is that girls respond equally well to learning techniques that take these needs into account whereas a proportion of the boys will see their results suffer if lessons require them to be more self-directing.'

So does this mean that group-based learning that requires children to pursue their own line of questioning puts boys at an advantage?

'There is no categorical answer to that. All I can say is that it puts a proportion of the boys at a disadvantage, but this flattens out when the curriculum as a whole is taken into account. What does appear to be true is that on the whole girls have superior verbal skills whereas boys score better on fact-based multiple-choice testing.'

There is certainly a school of thought, and a vocal lobby group, that claims that modern teaching methods promote the interests of girls above those of boys. Statistically, girls are outperforming boys in many subjects and attain a higher percentage of available university places. Before anyone raising boys panics and demands a return to rote learning and regular exams, it's worth looking at how those statistics turn around as the years go by. Girls may be doing better than boys at school, but when it comes to rates of pay and their share of the domestic burden, it certainly does appear that men are still running the world.

'I HAVE A BOY AND A GIRL WHO BUCK THE STEREOTYPES WHEN IT COMES TO SCHOOL. JOSH IS INCREDIBLY ARTICULATE, LOVES PUBLIC SPEAKING AND WRITING. HE TAKES REAL PLEASURE IN EXPLORING ABSTRACT CONCEPTS AND AS FAR AS HE'S CONCERNED READING AND WRITING STORIES IS WHERE IT'S AT – HE'S A LOT LIKE ME. ROSE IS HER DAD ALL OVER – IF YOU CAN'T PROVE IT, SHE DOESN'T WANT TO KNOW ABOUT IT.'

The principal was much more explicit about the gender split when it comes to disciplinary problems, especially bullying. 'The clichés are true when it comes to behavioural problems. On the whole girls bully girls and boys stick to other boys. You do see cases where bullying crosses gender lines but it's pretty rare. When girls bully it tends to be verbal and to revolve around excluding and belittling the victim. With boys, on the other hand, it's almost always physical.

'One thing that isn't affected by gender is the impact that bullying has on the victim, it's equally devastating for boys and girls. Where differences do arise it tends to revolve around how apparent, or not, the bullying is. It's pretty hard to disguise physical bullying, not impossible, obviously, but difficult. Bullying between girls tends to be verbal and when you combine that with their heightened verbal abilities, it's much easier for girls to maintain a culture of silence and that in turn can make it harder for parents and the school to take action.'

Exclusion and belittlement are potent weapons and can have a lasting effect on a victim's self-esteem. While early intervention can head off sustained damage, it can't be relied upon. The best defence against bullies is confidence, both physical and emotional. Self-esteem is a much-abused term (and there are some who think too much can be as dangerous as too little), but there is no denying that a little confidence can go a long way when it comes to psychological defence. It's not simply a question of how you go about instilling confidence, but whether different techniques are required for your sons and daughters.

I figured this was a good time to consult the experts and the response was unanimous. When it comes to boosting your children's confidence with direct techniques such as praise, rewards or understanding, boys and girls respond equally and positively to all of the methods. Where it got tricky was the consensus that our actions have as much, if not more, of an impact. Not the easy stuff like the way we treat our children, that would be too easy, but the way we treat our partner, friends, family and, most importantly, the way we treat ourselves. This has an enormous impact on the way our children see themselves.

One of the trickiest areas, especially when it comes to mothers and daughters, is body image. The way we treat our own bodies and the way we talk about them has an immediate knock-on effect on our daughters at their most impressionable. Getting a handle on our attitude to our shape, or lack of it, is bloody tricky. Hands up if you actually like your body? Right, now let's hear from those of you who are actually prepared to flaunt it. Finally, hands up if you can hardly bring yourself to look in the mirror naked. Mmm, me too.

So let's do the checklist. Do I eat well? Try to. Exercise? Yep, not enough, but I make an effort. Criticise myself constantly and unthinkingly? Yep, that's me. So on the one hand I'm careful to treat my daughter's body with the utmost respect. I praise it, pamper it and do my best to take care of it. On the other hand she has grown up hearing me say, 'God, I feel so fat!' on an almost daily basis, and that's the mild stuff. Examine a tough day, the day before my period, say, or after a big meal, and I can get seriously vicious. I'm not totally stupid, and I'd bite my tongue before I said these things to her, or even consciously in front of her. Get me on the phone, or deep in conversation with a girlfriend and the insults fly thick and fast. It's like I assume that if I'm not directly communicating with her, she can't hear me, but of course she can, and every little barb I throw at myself hits the mark with her as well.

'I JUST NEVER STOPPED TO THINK ABOUT HOW MUCH OF MY ATTITUDE TO MYSELF WAS HITTING HOME WITH MOLLY. I CAN BE SERIOUSLY HARD ON MYSELF AND WHEN I'M WITH MY SISTER WE'LL REALLY LET RIP, COMPARING ARSE SIZES, SHOWING OFF OUR FLABBY STOMACHS AND STRETCH MARKS. WE PRETEND IT'S ALL IN FUN, BUT, WELL, IT'S HARD TO FEEL GOOD ABOUT YOUR BODY AFTER YOU'VE POPPED OUT A COUPLE OF KIDS. ONE DAY, WHEN MOLLY WAS ABOUT NINE, SHE HAD A GIRLFRIEND OVER. THEY WERE EATING WATERMELON ON THE TRAMPOLINE. I WAS WATERING THE GARDEN AND KIND OF HALF-LISTENING, WHEN MOLLY SAID, "I'D LOVE ANOTHER PIECE, BUT I'M HAVING A FAT DAY". I WANTED TO CRY, NOT JUST BECAUSE IT WAS SO RIDICULOUS, BUT BECAUSE SHE SOUNDED JUST LIKE ME.'

It's impossible to continually self-censor; no one is a saint and my checklist of things to do and not do is so overwhelming I can hardly face the idea of adding yet another task. This one, though, is really worth it. Rarely has 'practise what you preach' been more relevant. What's the point in preaching acceptance of yourself and others if you are engaged in a war of attrition with your own self-esteem? You never know, lay off your arse for a while and it might even get smaller, or at least appear to.

Getting back to baby boys in pink pyjamas, and there are few sights cuter than that one, it's now as clear as mud to me that gender both matters, and doesn't matter. You can't turn a tomboy into a glamour puss or a mini-snag into a rugger-bugger. You can, however, in a perfect world, allow your children to be distinct individuals while making allowances in style according to both need and gender. At least, I've heard that you can. Those of you smart enough to crack the code are hereby bound by the conventions of motherhood to spread the word, clearly, concisely and, preferably, loudly.

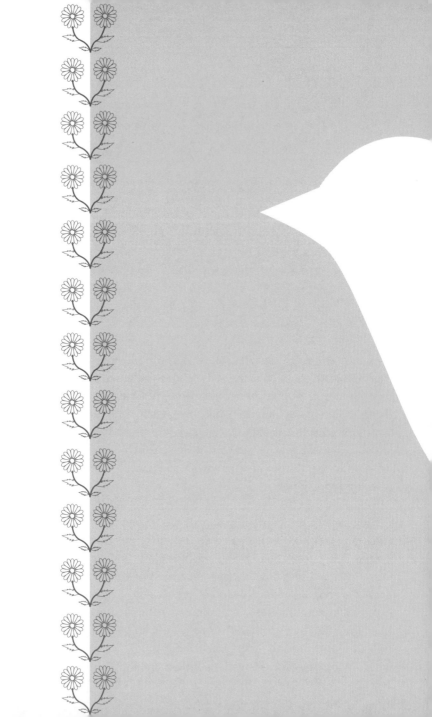

More than you
can chew

'YOU MAY BE DECEIVED IF YOU
TRUST TOO MUCH, BUT YOU WILL
LIVE IN TORMENT IF YOU DON'T
TRUST ENOUGH.'

FRANK CRANE

Telling the truth

'If you do not tell the truth about yourself, you cannot tell it about other people.'

VIRGINIA WOOLF

There's a lot more to telling the truth than simply not lying. When it comes to kids and relationships, lying, or rather, not lying, is a good place to start. Lying is a funny old thing; we all do it but few of us will admit to it. We have different standards when it comes to telling the truth and many of us have elastic standards depending on the situation or even the method of communication. White lies and excuses are easy for some, especially on email or via SMS, but none of us would even contemplate wide-eyed and chocolate-smeared denial in the face of missing Easter eggs. Until the day we're faced with requests for the hard truths, the ones about sex and drugs and rock and roll.

I was cruising down the highway of easygoing motherhood; we'd had one of those extraordinary months when it appeared that everyone was happy and everything was easy. We were driving across town early one morning when our eldest child suddenly piped up. He wanted an answer to a really simple question: where babies come from. I'd always arrogantly assumed I'd ace this one when it came my way. I'm pretty open-minded and firmly believe that accurate information is the least you owe your children. So it came as something of a shock to discover I had no more stomach for talking about sex at 8 am on a rainy Tuesday than I had for having it (at 8 am on a busy, rainy Tuesday, that is). I just brushed him off with a vague and rambling answer and then used the tried-and-tested distraction technique of calling out, 'Who can see the Harbour Bridge?'. Failing so pathetically at the first step got me thinking: how was I going to handle it when the questions got really tough? Would I chicken out when it came to explaining death? What about mental illness or drug abuse? Few of our lives are untouched by drama and tragedy, so when do we pull our punches, and when is it time to tell the unvarnished truth?

TRUTH IN PARENTING

'WHEN MY MARRIAGE BROKE DOWN MY FIRST PRIORITY WAS TO MAKE SURE THAT EVERYTHING WAS DONE IN THE BEST POSSIBLE WAY FOR THE KIDS. IT'S NEVER GOING TO BE EASY TELLING YOUR CHILDREN THAT YOU ARE SEPARATING, BUT WE GOT ADVICE AND I THINK WE HANDLED IT PRETTY WELL. WHAT I DIDN'T ANTICIPATE WAS HOW HARD IT WAS MANAGING MY EMOTIONS WITHOUT LETTING THEM IMPACT ON THE KIDS. I FELT LIKE I WAS MOURNING IN SECRET, AND THE ONLY TIME I COULD LET MY OWN PAIN OUT WAS WHEN THEY WERE WITH THEIR DAD.

'THERE WERE A COUPLE OF HAIRY DAYS WHEN I HONESTLY DIDN'T KNOW IF I COULD MAKE IT THROUGH ANOTHER DAY PRETENDING TO BE CHEERFUL. I WISH I COULD HAVE FOUND A WAY TO BE MORE OPEN WITH THEM, BUT AT THE TIME THERE JUST DIDN'T SEEM TO BE ONE.'

Truth in parenting can be a little like truth in politics, a malleable entity that needs to be massaged and finessed depending on your constituency. Communicating the raw truth can be the only honourable thing to do when you're dealing with a teenager. Degrees of detail are more or less appropriate depending on the age of the child you're dealing with, but this gets sticky when you need to impart differing levels of information on the same subject to siblings of varying ages. While asking an older child to respect the innocence of their younger siblings can offer a level of privilege and confidence, it can also place a burden of silence on a child who may already be struggling with the information you've given them. It can also cause friction between siblings once it becomes apparent you've told them a different story.

When I was in my late teens, my family, like most at some time, was visited by tragedy. My mother's sister died a very untimely and devastating death. The four of us, my siblings and I, are seven years apart from end to end. I was 17 when it happened, and telling me the whole truth was the automatic choice for my parents. My younger sister, on the other hand, was only ten and I guess they felt the need to protect her from some of the details. I don't know how they went about it, but they did a fantastic job, as it wasn't until we were both adults that we discovered we'd carried different versions of our aunt's death with us for all those years.

HALF-TRUTHS

Sometimes the circumstances of events collide with the age of your children in a way that relieves you of the burden of assessing how to handle it. 'Lachlan was eight and Greta was only a baby when my husband first began to display real signs of mental illness,' says

Jamaica. 'Bipolar is an incredibly difficult disease to manage, and really hard to hide. There was no way I could fully protect Lachie from what was happening, and though we discussed it in a way that he could relate to, he didn't really want to talk about it that much. With Greta it's been different – easier and harder. We live in a different city now and she has a stepfather she thinks of as her father. While she knows Len is her biological father, Pat is her "dad" and she almost never talks about Len.' Jamaica has taken full responsibility for making sure that both of her children spend time with their father, but it is time that needs to be carefully supervised. 'It can be a scary illness; he won't medicate the disease so he's not really capable of taking responsibility for their safety. It's also a scary thing to talk about, so far, I just haven't felt like Greta is old enough. This is something we will get around to talking about, just not yet.'

'JAMILA IS SUCH AN INCREDIBLY DREAMY CHILD AND SEEMS TO LIVE IN ANOTHER WORLD MOST OF THE TIME. SHE WRITES THE MOST BEAUTIFUL STORIES, BUT DOESN'T SEEM TO REALLY UNDERSTAND THE LINE BETWEEN TRUTH AND FICTION. WHEN SHE'S DEEPLY INVOLVED IN A STORY, IT'S ALMOST LIKE SHE STARTS TO LIVE INSIDE IT. THE NEIGHBOURS HAVE GOT USED TO HER BEING "ADOPTED" ONE WEEK AND AN "OPERA STAR" THE NEXT, BUT I'VE HAD TO DO SOME FAIRLY TRICKY EXPLAINING AT SCHOOL. WE JUST HOPE SHE DECIDES SHE WANTS TO BE AN AUTHOR AND NOT A LAWYER!'

The very fact that children are so adept at blurring the line between fact and fiction makes it doubly important for us, as their parents, to communicate the truth appropriately and sensitively. Half-truths can be more dangerous than the whole and unadulterated version, no matter how sticky the details may be. There is a reason witnesses are asked, when taking the stand, to tell 'the truth, the whole truth and nothing but the truth'. Accuracy is not just in the details, it's also contained within the breadth of information given. Sometimes the most difficult, and painful, aspect of the truth is contained within the detail, yet skirting around that detail can be surprisingly easy.

'We were all in the car heading south when Jess hit us with the big one,' says Amanda. 'She was halfway through kindergarten and starting to hear the big kids talking about sex. I always planned to be open and honest about it, but I never expected to get the kind of questions she was asking. There were things that I would never, ever have asked my mother. So we're driving along, Joe's driving and Jess and Sarah are sitting in the back staring out the window. I was watching them in the little mirror in the sun visor, they both looked really sweet and innocent, just out of bed, sun shining on their faces. Jess saw me looking at her and decided this was a great time to hit me for some more information. She's pretty smart and I think she knew that tackling me in the car would make it harder for me to worm my way out of it.

'"So, Mum," she started, "I know that sex is just a whole lot of lovin', but there has to be more to it than that." Joe gave me a look; I'd told him about Jessie's questions and he'd thought the whole thing was pretty funny, until now.

'"Yeah," I said, "of course there's more to it, but I thought we'd worked that out already."

'"Mmmm," she thinks for a moment, "I know that the daddy puts his penis in the mummy's vagina." Suddenly Joe's hands tighten on the wheel. "But once it's in there," Jess continued, "does he move it around or does it just stay still?"

'"Well,' I said, "he moves it around," attempting to make it sound really casual.

'Jess stares out of the window for a moment and then hits us with, "So, Mum, when Dad puts his penis in your vagina …" but then Joe swerves into another lane, car horns blast and I stick a story CD in the player. Jess never got to finish the question, but in a way I think she'd got her answer.'

'ON NEW YEAR'S EVE WHEN WE WERE ALL WALKING UP THE HILL TO WATCH THE FIREWORKS, KITTY WAS HOLDING MY HAND AND AN OLDER WOMAN WALKING ALONGSIDE US HAD JUST GIVEN ME THAT "OH, ISN'T SHE CUTE?" LOOK WHEN KITTY SAID, VERY LOUDLY, "MUMMY, DADDY HAS A PENIS."

'I WENT BRIGHT RED AND TRIED TO BE CASUAL AND JOLLY AND JUST SAID, "YES DARLING, THAT'S RIGHT, ALL DADDIES HAVE A PENIS."

'"MMM," SAID KITTY, "BUT MY DADDY HAS A BIG PENIS WITH HAIR ON IT." MOP OF BLONDE CURLS NOTWITHSTANDING, I CAN GUARANTEE THAT THE WOMAN ALONGSIDE US NO LONGER THOUGHT KITTY WAS CUTE, IN FACT, IT'S A WONDER SHE DIDN'T CALL SOCIAL SERVICES.'

THE INFORMATION REVOLUTION

Children are bombarded with information these days, that much is true, but then so are we. They may well be much more worldly than we were at their age, but I wouldn't be surprised if the same was true for us as adults. Western history traces a path through a series of revolutions: the agrarian revolution, the industrial revolution, the French and American ones, and most recently, the information revolution. We have become the daily receptors of a greater amount of information than our forebears could even have imagined. The tyranny of distance has been truly conquered; daily email dispatches are the record of a world journey and the six-month wait for news of loved ones almost lost to human memory. Some of us can be prone to fits of panic if our loved ones are out of range for more than a day. Imagine the mindset of a mother who waved her son off to the new world and then had to wait six months for news of his safe arrival. Information now arrives instantly and constantly and the web of communication that binds us together has become an intrinsic part of daily life.

Personal communication is only one aspect of the information revolution. We have also become the repositories of vast amounts of impersonal information – from wars to the sex lives of celebrities – so little remains hidden from our eyes and ears, and by extension, those of our children. It can come as a nasty shock the first time you discover that your child knows an awful lot more than you anticipated, or desired. Hard as they were to answer at the time, those early questions about sex came out of ignorance and innocence and left you free to fill in the blanks in the way you saw fit. As your child matures, their knowledge is like a jigsaw puzzle with mismatched pieces, missing corners and no picture to work from – you have to work out what you're dealing with before you can even begin to put it together. The name of the game is communication.

It's widely acknowledged that the key to a long-lasting relationship is communication. One old fellow who recently celebrated 60 years of wedded bliss claimed the success of his marriage lay in just two little words – 'Yes, dear'. It makes for a neat headline, but in most cases, it takes rather more than that to have a successful relationship. Without communication there is no relationship, you may as well be living with a stranger, and what goes in your marriage extends to your relationship with your children.

> 'AS FAR AS I'M CONCERNED, THE ONLY WAY TO HAVE RESPECT IN A RELATIONSHIP IS TO MAKE SURE IT GOES BOTH WAYS. I HAVE A DEAL WITH ELIZA WHERE SHE IS FREE TO CONFIDE ANYTHING IN ME AND, IN RETURN, I RESPECT THE WAY SHE WANTS IT TO BE DEALT WITH. IT'S NOT THAT I GIVE UP ALL INFLUENCE, TALKING ABOUT IT MEANS THAT I HAVE A LOT OF INFLUENCE, BUT AT THE END OF THE DAY, IF SHE FEELS REALLY STRONGLY ABOUT SOMETHING, I'M BOUND TO RESPECT THAT. SOME PEOPLE THINK IT'S A FAIRLY FULL-ON APPROACH TO TAKE WITH A SEVEN-YEAR-OLD, BUT WHAT I'M DOING IS LOOKING AHEAD. IF SHE'S 14 AND "UP THE DUFF" WE NEED TO HAVE A RELATIONSHIP WHERE SHE CAN COME TO ME ABOUT IT, AND I THINK THE BEST WAY TO MAKE THAT HAPPEN IS TO START BUILDING IT NOW.'

Keeping the lines of communication open is the most effective way to make sure that you don't miss out on the important stuff. There's nothing worse than being the last one to know and the later you find out what is going on, the less power you have to do something about the situation.

As an adolescent, Linda learnt some sobering lessons about the importance of the lines of communication between parents and children. 'When I was about 14 I went to a concert at the local hall; it was the mid-80s and the local music scene was split between surfer rock and the alternative New-Romantic scene. I was with a group of girls from school. We were up for a big night and to us that meant getting pissed. We'd all nicked a bottle of something from our parents' liquor cupboards and were buzzing by the time we hit the hall.

'THE WEB OF OUR LIFE IS OF A
MINGLED YARN, GOOD AND ILL
TOGETHER.'

WILLIAM SHAKESPEARE

'One of our number was beyond buzzy, she was flat-out wasted, to the point that she seemed out of control even to us. We did our best to look after her, taking it in turns to chaperone her through the night, but we weren't up to the job and in the end we lost control of the situation. Our friend disappeared, and in the early hours of the morning the police found her wandering disorientated in a local park. She had been raped and, as friends, we had failed her.'

From an adult perspective, the obvious question is why nobody called in a parent. 'Maybe things are different now. For a start, this was before the days of mobile phones so making a call was not an automatic thing to do. But I think it's more that phoning a parent was a last resort, it was a scary thing to do because, to us, it just led to trouble. That night we all learnt the hard way that there are worse ways of getting into trouble. When my kids were old enough, I told them this story and said, "No matter how bad things seem, getting a grown-up you trust on the scene will make things better. If you can't call anyone else, call me, no matter who is in trouble, and I'll do my best to sort it out." So far, they haven't needed to, but they know that I am here for all of them at any time. More than anything, I think it was embarrassment and fear that stopped any of us calling our parents. How stupid is that?'

Telling the truth can be embarrassing, in fact, a lot of lies are told in the vain hope of avoiding embarrassment. Well, the day you gave birth you were letting yourself in for what seems like a lifetime of embarrassment, so you may as well get used to it. Recently, I asked the mother of one of Will's friends if she would take him home after school so that I could finally get on with finishing this book. She agreed, and I said to Will, 'You can go for a play at Toby's house now, isn't that lovely?'. Well, apparently it wasn't.

'I don't want to go to Toby's,' said Will, 'What about Bertie? Can you call his mum, or Alex, or Fred?' He went on and on; I ended up taking him by the arm and hauling him out of the schoolyard red with embarrassment. I should be used to it by now, but I'm not and I probably never will be. I have, however, made a solemn promise to myself that embarrassment will never stop me from telling my kids the truth.

'POPPY WAS THREE WHEN I GOT PREGNANT WITH THE TWINS AND WAS RIGHT IN THE MIDDLE OF THE "MUM, WHY DOES ..." STAGE. I LOVED HER CURIOSITY AND WANTED TO TELL HER AS MUCH AS I COULD ABOUT THE WHOLE THING. I WENT AND BOUGHT AN ARMFUL OF BOOKS TO HELP PREPARE FIRST-BORNS FOR LIFE WITH A BROTHER OR SISTER AND A GREAT BOOK ON PREGNANCY AND BIRTH FOR PRESCHOOLERS. THE WHOLE THING WAS REALLY COSY; WE'D SNUGGLE DOWN WITH A COUPLE OF BOOKS AND I'D ALWAYS SLIP IN ONE ABOUT SOMEONE'S BABY BROTHER, OR MUMMY'S TUMMY OR WHATEVER.

'WE'D ALREADY BEEN THROUGH THE FASCINATION-WITH-GENITALS THING AND SOMEHOW POPPY HAD SETTLED ON THE WORD "BADGER" FOR VAGINA. SHE WAS REALLY TAKEN WITH THE IDEA THAT THE BABIES WOULD COME OUT OF MY BADGER, AND FELT THE NEED TO ASK A LOT OF QUESTIONS ABOUT IT, BEFORE SHE SUDDENLY SEEMED TO LOSE INTEREST IN THE WHOLE THING.

'A MONTH OR SO LATER, WE WERE AT THE SUPERMARKET UNLOADING THE TROLLEY. BY THIS STAGE I WAS IN MY EIGHTH MONTH AND COMPLETELY ENORMOUS. I BENT OVER THE TROLLEY TO GET SOMETHING OUT AND HAD ONE OF THOSE STABBING LIGAMENT PAINS THAT MAKES YOU CRY OUT. THE PLACE WAS PACKED, AND I GOT THE ODD CONCERNED LOOK BUT I WAS PRETTY GOOD BY NOW AT MAKING IT CLEAR THAT EVERYTHING WAS FINE WITHOUT SAYING A WORD. NEXT THING I KNOW,

POPPY PIPES UP, IN A VERY CLEAR, VERY LOUD VOICE, "OH NO, MUMMY,
IS YOUR BADGER STRETCHING TO LET THE BABIES OUT?".'

I've yet to meet a mother who has escaped unscathed, which makes for a delicious collection of war stories. I love the weird and wonderful things kids say to you; it's one of the best things about being a mother. Like the other day my daughter was sitting on the front step staring off into space with this really dreamy look on her face. Just as I was wondering what she was thinking about she turned to me and said, 'Mummy, all childrens are vanilla'. I loved that one and put it down in the wonderful column, but sometimes they come out with things that are so weird they can freak you out.

'It's important to remember that we underestimate our kids,' says Sarah. 'When my oldest boy, Jack, was five and his younger brother, Sam, was almost three, Jack was going through a stage of being fascinated and afraid of death. He was constantly asking questions about it, especially about the fact that everyone dies. One day we were driving along listening to Jack explain that it was all okay as even though everyone dies they don't die till they're 100. Out of the blue Sam announced, "Well, I'm going to die when I'm three."

'Feeling a bit shocked, I said, "Oh, darling, I hope not, because I'd be really sad if you died when you were three."

'"I wouldn't be sad," said Sam, "because then I'd find the new key to unlock this cage that I'm kept in." I actually had to pull the car over to the side of the road. Even though I know what I heard, I still can't believe such a small child could say something so bizarre and profound and I never, ever assume that I know what's going on in my children's heads.'

Death is one of the tough ones when it comes to communicating truthfully with our kids. For a start, many of us have little experience of dealing with death and when it does enter our lives, we are in the midst of trying to process our own grief. Very small children find the concept of death itself incredibly hard to understand. When our cat died, I assumed that the kids would be devastated. They had really loved The Chairman, cuddled him, dressed him and fussed over him, and now they had lost a beloved pet to a busy road. Our neighbour found The Chairman's battered body on the side of the road during the school day, so I had hours to prepare how I was going to tell them about it.

I consulted friends, rang my husband, girded my loins and then sat them down and gently broke the news. The shocking thing for me was that they couldn't have been less affected by the news. They just shrugged it off and went back to watchng Play School. When my husband got home I confided that I suspected our children might actually be entirely heartless. 'Don't be stupid,' he said, 'they just don't know what dead means.' So he dug a grave, arranged the cat's body as tastefully as possible and then conducted a funeral service with the kids. It was sad and moving. When the children saw The Chairman's body they reacted with real sadness. He was so obviously lifeless that the meaning of death was apparent. They shed a few tears, put his toys in the hole and helped cover him over. Conducting a ceremony gave them a chance to gain real insight into the meaning of death and an opportunity to talk about how they felt.

Dealing with the death of someone, especially a family member, is something all parents will face sooner or later. Grandparents die, so do parents, friends, and, in some heartbreaking situations, siblings. When Kate's daughter died in the family home, she found herself having to manage her own grief and that of her remaining children.

'Finding Melissa was the worst moment of my entire life,' she says. 'Having to tell Kirsty came a close second. I could hardly speak, I was so consumed with pain, but I knew that we, Chris and I, had to tell her together that her sister was dead.'

> *'Making a decision to have a child – it's momentous. It is to decide forever to have your heart go walking outside your body.'*
>
> ELIZABETH SCOTT

The death of a child is every parent's worst nightmare. We are lucky enough to be bringing our children up at a time in history when they are more likely to reach adulthood than ever before. As a community we no longer have a social understanding of what it means to lose a child; we have lost access to the comfort of a communal truth. Kate was required, in the middle of profound grief and pain, to search for her own truths in order to communicate them to her children. 'I don't know if I would have survived this if I hadn't had to keep going for Kirsty,' she says. 'Being there for her meant that I couldn't just turn away from life. All I wanted to do after Melissa died was curl up in a ball and pretend that nothing had happened, or I just wanted to die. But I couldn't, I had to be present, I had to search for my own truth, my faith and strength. Without it, I would have had nothing to give my daughter who was still alive.' The truth is a poor substitute for a sibling, but it was the best that Kate could offer. 'I needed to help her to understand what it meant for Mel to be dead.'

Acknowledging difficult truths doesn't prevent you from finding palatable ways to express them. When Nina's brother-in-law committed suicide she felt she needed to find a way to tell her children that offered comfort as well as honesty. 'After we told the boys about Peter's death I felt really strongly that we needed to find a happy way to remember him,' she says. 'Death is always horrible but one of the worst things about suicide is the madness that comes before it. Pete had been progressively delusional before he died and it had been hard to protect the boys from that. I wanted to find something that would kind of override the hideous memories. After we told the boys what had happened, we went outside and looked up at the night sky. The boys chose a star and we decided that star was where Pete had gone. Every night for years afterwards, we'd go outside and say goodnight to Uncle Pete before the boys went to bed.'

'WHEN MY HUSBAND AND I SEPARATED WE WERE REALLY HONEST WITH THE KIDS ABOUT WHAT WAS GOING ON. WE TRIED TO KEEP THEM FULLY INFORMED AND WERE COMMITTED TO ANSWERING ANY QUESTIONS THEY HAD. BECAUSE THEY SEEMED OKAY ABOUT IT I ASSUMED THAT THEY WERE. ON THE DAY THAT PAUL MOVED OUT WE HELPED HIM PACK THE CAR AND THE PLAN WAS THAT THE KIDS WOULD GO OVER WITH HIM AND HELP PUT A FEW THINGS IN THE NEW PLACE. I AGREED TO PICK THEM UP AT FIVE AND OFF THEY WENT. WHEN I CAME AROUND TO GET THEM, THEY WERE FINE UNTIL IT WAS TIME TO LEAVE. LILY WAS ONLY FIVE AT THE TIME AND SHE JUST COULDN'T UNDERSTAND WHY PAUL WASN'T COMING HOME WITH US. ALL THE TALKING WE'D DONE AND I'D ASSUMED THAT THE DIFFICULTY WOULD BE IN HOW THEY TOOK IT, NOT IN WHETHER OR NOT THEY'D EVEN UNDERSTOOD WHAT WAS GOING ON.'

It would be a mistake to ever assume that we know what's going on in anyone else's head, let alone our children's. We also can't assume that they understand the intended meaning of the information they receive, especially when they're still really young. My mother-in-law took the boys to the museum when they were three and five. While absorbed in one of the exhibitions she managed to lose the younger one, without even realising it (you can imagine how much I loved hearing this story for the first time!). In fact, she was unaware that Will was missing until there was an announcement over the PA system that went like this, 'We have a lost child at security on the second floor. His name is Will, he's three years old and he's wearing a red jumper. Would his parents please come and collect him'.

Liza thought to herself, 'Oh, that sounds like my Will', she looked around and, realising it was her Will, made her way to security.

When she got there, Will was happily sitting on a chair shooting the breeze with the guards. 'Hello, Granny,' he said.

'Hello, Will,' she replied. 'Let's go.'

'I can't,' said Will, 'I'm waiting for my parents to collect me.' Will had heard the announcement but wasn't old enough to put it into context. In order to properly communicate with our children we need to know where they are at and the only way to know that is to listen.

Tackling the tough stuff can be a balancing act between wanting to protect their innocence and giving them the tools to protect themselves. The abduction of children by strangers is one of the spectres that haunts every parent's imagination, the possibility that a deranged individual could snatch your precious child away. Drawing the line between instilling caution and creating unnecessary fear is not easy; taking a commonsense approach and using plain language is probably the best starting point. In some ways parenthood is like a conversation that lasts a lifetime. There are so many things we want to teach them, so much we can learn from them, so many new adventures to undertake together. Keep it open, keep it honest and you can tackle anything that comes your way.

'Everything's got a moral, if only you can find it.'

LEWIS CARROLL

'ONLY WHEN WE ARE NO LONGER
AFRAID DO WE BEGIN TO LIVE.'

DOROTHY THOMPSON

Playing it safe

'Don't be afraid to go out on a limb. That's where the fruit is.'

H. JACKSON BROWNE

When I was a kid, there were at least 20 other kids living in my street. When we all tumbled home from school, walking on our own, the last thing our mums wanted was for us to be hanging around the house getting in the way. Unless it was pouring with rain, and the lightning was dangerously close, you could forget about sitting down in front of the television. Playstations hadn't been invented, although Pacman was just on the horizon. I think that, looking back through hazy memory, one boy on the street had that black-and-white tennis game. We were expected to play outside and entertain ourselves and, so long as we were home for dinner, no one even thought to ask where we were going. Not that we would have been able to tell them as we all got on our bikes and headed off to roam around. Sometimes we went to the tennis courts, sometimes the playground, but most of the time we just built magnificently complicated and dangerous tunnel-forts in the bush out the back. We'd come home dirty, tired and often injured (though stitches were only required twice). Would I let my kids do the same thing? Not on your life; I wish I could but things have changed and the business of play is much more complicated now.

Bucking the system isn't easy; one friend, Lissa, lives all of 100 m from the local school with one road to cross on the way, conveniently guarded by a zebra crossing. The thought of letting Jacinta walk to school on her own is tempting, but so far, Lissa has resisted the urge. 'On Saturday mornings, however, Jacinta has ballet in the school hall,' says Lissa, 'and she pestered the hell out of me to let her walk by herself. I've got two-year-old twins as well, and nine on a Saturday morning is not the best time for any of us. Joe, my husband, is much more inclined to let Jac do her own thing, and he finally convinced me that walking on her own would be fine. So we let her go, got the twins ready and followed about 45 minutes later to pick her up and go for breakfast. I'd been pretty nervous about letting her go, but figured that it was only around the corner, and she's nearly seven, so I was probably just being ridiculous. By the time we got there, Joe and I were actually congratulating ourselves on having evolved enough as parents to give Jacinta the trust and tools she needs to tackle life.

'Well, that was pretty short-lived. I went in to pick up Jac, and the teacher leapt straight at me. She couldn't believe we'd let Jacinta do it, essentially accused me of neglect and said that unless she was properly escorted, she couldn't do the class.'

In retrospect the thing that annoys Lissa the most isn't that someone else felt they had the authority to countermand her parenting decisions, but that Lissa let it happen. 'Afterwards I thought, "In what way is it up to her? And why the hell did I let her do that?".' The line between freedom and safety is a work in progress that develops as children do. It is also a part of parenting that has gone from being a private judgment to a public bone of contention.

When it comes to the safety of children, parents are damned if they do and damned if they don't. Arrayed on one side are the interventionists who insist that parents have a duty to monitor their children at all times; they see danger lurking in every corner and behind every hedge. In their eyes parents are not only responsible for guarding their children, they are also capable of preventing any harm from befalling the littlies. Should they ever get organised enough to march through the streets, their banners would read, 'There is no such thing as an accident' and 'Blame works'. Looking on in scorn from the opposing side are the autonomists, who believe that children denied the freedom to roam around their environment unhindered are not only profoundly deprived but actively prevented from developing into fully self-sufficient human beings. Their banners may well read, 'Liberty for the littlies' and 'Free the minors'. Caught in the middle is an increasingly bewildered mass of parents trying to incorporate their duty of care with their children's right to self-determination.

INDEPENDENCE

Trying to balance concerns about safety with your child's natural drive for independence is not helped by the regular bouts of hysteria that afflict public debate over matters of private safety. There's more than enough hysteria involved in the daily routine without someone bringing in a nasty dose from the outside. Deliberately negligent, or even harmful, parents are rightly reviled yet relatively rare. Most of us do our best, even with limited means, to ensure that our children are protected from unnecessary harm. It's a short step, but a long fall, from taking measures designed to protect to descending into a paranoid state whereby every object, substance and person is dangerous until proven otherwise.

'ABOUT 38 WEEKS INTO MY PREGNANCY I DECIDED THAT IT WAS TIME TO BABY-PROOF THE HOUSE. I INSTALLED SAFETY GATES, PLUG COVERS AND A LOCK ON THE LOO SEAT AND FELT VERY PROUD AND PREPARED. I COULDN'T HAVE ANTICIPATED THE STATE OF ALARM I FELL INTO WHEN I FIRST GOT LAURA HOME. I WAS AFRAID OF HER BEING HURT BY JUST ABOUT EVERY OBJECT IN THE HOUSE. ONE NIGHT I EVEN MADE MY HUSBAND GET UP AT TWO IN THE MORNING AND DRAG THE WARDROBE OUT OF OUR ROOM 'COS I'D BECOME CONVINCED IT COULD FALL AND CRUSH HER WHILE WE WERE SLEEPING. IT GOT TO THE POINT WHERE I WOULDN'T VISIT MY PARENTS ANY MORE BECAUSE OF THEIR COFFEE TABLE. IT WAS THIS RUSTIC WOODEN COFFEE TABLE WITH ROUGH EDGES AND SHARP CORNERS. BEAR IN MIND THAT LAURA WASN'T EVEN OLD ENOUGH TO SIT UP YET, BUT I'D FIND MYSELF STARING AT THE CORNERS AND ACTUALLY FEELING NAUSEOUS AT THE IMAGE OF HER SMASHING HER HEAD ON THEM.'

Humans, as a species, have a vested interest in keeping their offspring alive. Above and beyond the fragile matter of love, there is the propagation of the species to be accomplished, and species that neglect their children swiftly become non-species. I don't want to spend yet another chapter qualifying every opinion I hold by stating that it is, of course, entirely possible that the opposite may be true, or that there are exceptions to the rule. I'm going to assume that you are intelligent enough to insert your own qualifiers and experienced enough to sift everything you read through the mesh of this world's overwhelming complexity. So if you should stumble across the odd categorical statement while navigating this chapter, please assume that I have taken into account, but decided not to mention, the odd glaring exception to the rule. I'm also going to assume that you are fully aware that there are certain things that, as a parent, you must categorically and under all circumstances do, or not do, depending on what that thing is. A few examples for the confused: drive a car under the influence of alcohol or drugs, with or without your children in it; go to Spain for a fortnight and leave your children to fend for themselves; allow your child to drive a car, whether or not they are under the influence of alcohol or drugs; you get the picture.

On top of this, I'm going to assume that should you and I have a difference of opinion we are both big enough to handle it and, that if not, the chances are we wouldn't be friends anyway. I am going to hereby assert that I will not be held liable for anybody feeling that I have in any way oversimplified, overcomplicated or ignored any aspect of parenthood.

The publishers are quite keen on me mentioning that all opinions and assertions within this book are the work of the author (that's me) and do not reflect the opinion of the publisher (which does, anyway, require you to confuse a company with a sentient being). The author hereby divests herself of any responsibility for your enjoyment or not of the finished product and furthermore asserts that any and every idea and action you have is entirely your own responsibility and does not implicate the author in any way or at any time. Finally, the author would like to remind you that your life is inherently risky and you should therefore lock your doors and take all valuables with you, as no responsibility will be taken by anybody, for anything, because it's all your fault anyway.

.

There you go; I've managed to take all of the possible risk entailed by anybody but you out of the above paragraph, and at the same time, all of the fun. And the chances are I haven't even achieved that as I'm sure that even an average lawyer could find a way to make it my fault. The point is, of course, that risk is inherent in everything we do, even in sitting down at a computer and writing a few words. We cannot remove all traces of risk from our children's lives, and we would, in fact, be negligent if we did. Forget about the ubiquitous chicken, how does a child cross the road if she never learns to cross the road? There comes a day when we are compelled by the marching years to let go of their hand, and unless we've allowed them to encounter and overcome risk along the way, we leave them defenceless.

Back when I was a kid we really did, in some ways, live free and unrestricted lives compared to our offspring. When my mother was 16 she and a girlfriend spent a week of every holiday cycling around the Lake District. They'd pitch a tent each evening and cycle on in the morn. When I was a kid, we'd get on our bikes after school and head off bound only by the need to be back at 5.30 for dinner. Our favourite activity was tunnelling; we'd spend hours digging elaborate tunnels in the bushland out the back, shoring them up with scrap iron, and then conducting guerrilla warfare against the builders of rival tunnels. My kids go to yoga class, art class, soccer, tennis and the local café.

'WE ARE LUCKY ENOUGH TO LIVE ON A QUIET STREET WITH BROAD FOOTPATHS. THERE ARE QUITE A FEW KIDS LIVING IN THE STREET AND THEY HAVE A CERTAIN AMOUNT OF FREEDOM. THEY CAN WALK BETWEEN EACH OTHER'S HOUSES UNESCORTED AND RIDE THEIR BIKES FROM END TO END. THERE ARE EVEN SOME TREES FOR THEM TO CLIMB, THOUGH IT'S A STRUGGLE NOT TO WINCE WHEN THEY REACH

THE HIGHER BRANCHES. WHEN FRIENDS VISIT THEY COMMENT ON HOW
LUCKY THE KIDS ARE TO HAVE SO MUCH FREEDOM, AND I FIND MYSELF
AGREEING, UNTIL I REMEMBER WHAT MY CHILDHOOD WAS LIKE. THE
FREEDOM OF ONE STREET IS PRETTY PALTRY BY COMPARISON.'

I have no intention of simply having a rant about how much better
things were way back when. The glow of nostalgia all too easily
obstructs the view of reality; if we are to wax lyrical about the good
times, we are bound also to acknowledge the bad and remember why
the changes came about in the first place. It's easy to remember that
we were largely allowed to go where we liked and easy to forget how
many of us were banned from thinking what we liked. Our children
are a generation that has lost a large amount of physical freedom, but
they have gained an enormous emotional and intellectual freedom
compared to their parents, grandparents and great-grandparents.

Let's start with the physical. There's no denying that today's children
enjoy an increased level of physical safety. It may have come at the
expense of physical freedom but it has also accorded children a level
of physical respect they have never before experienced. Simply put,
we no longer beat our children on a regular basis, we are no longer
complicit, in our silence, in the sexual and physical abuse of our
young. We are not perfect but we are determined to ensure that as
many children as possible are safe from harm tonight. If that comes
at the expense of a certain loss of freedom, strength and
independence, surely it's a valid trade-off. Well, actually, that depends
on who you are and how you look at it.

A mother who is also a doctor explains, 'As a parent I'm fairly
conscious of making sure my kids live a healthy life – not too much
television, plenty of vegies and fresh air. As a doctor, I'm acutely

aware that we are facing an epidemic of overweight and obese children. As a person I can remember that at my school there were only two fat kids, now there are more than that in every class.'

Avoiding unnecessary risk is part of being human; understanding and assessing risk accurately is a skill denied to most of us. Take flying as a classic example. Personally I'm not a massive fan of taking to the sky in a metal tube. There have been times when I've considered not attending a wedding or birthday because the thought of taking that risk once more is daunting. The thing that keeps me flying is simple: when I stand on the ground and see a plane fly overhead I have no expectation that it will crash, it makes sense for it to be in the air. On the other hand, I jump in my car without a second thought on an almost daily basis, and while I sometimes curse the stupidity of my fellow drivers, I don't drive along in a lather of fear. You don't need me to tell you how much more likely I am to die on the road than in the air, it's well known that driving is statistically much more dangerous, yet knowing is not the same as feeling.

If I were to allow my six-year-old to walk across the road and around the corner to the local park, spend an hour there and then come home, what are the chances he would come to any harm? I don't know and I don't care because I'm not going to let him do it and that's that. Whether that makes me stupid or simply obstinate, I don't know, but it does make me normal. I'm not alone in allowing instinct coloured by irrational fear to guide my decisions, in fact, it's getting crowded in here.

'WHENEVER I READ IN THE PAPER ABOUT SOMETHING DREADFUL HAPPENING TO A CHILD, I GET PARANOID THAT SOMETHING SIMILAR IS GOING TO HAPPEN TO ONE OF MINE. OCCASIONALLY, WHILE I'M DOING

SOMETHING MUNDANE LIKE STACKING THE DISHWASHER, I PLAY OUT
THESE COURTROOM SCENES IN MY HEAD WHERE I'M ON THE STAND
DEFENDING MYSELF FROM NEGLIGENCE. IT USUALLY GOES LIKE THIS,
"'SO, MRS JONES, WHERE WERE YOU WHEN YOUR DAUGHTER OPENED
THE FRONT DOOR AND LET HERSELF OUT?"

'ANXIOUS TEARS FROM ME, "I WAS GIVING THE BABY A BATH, YOUR
HONOUR."

"'OBJECTION!" YELLS OPPOSING COUNSEL. "THE FACT THAT MRS
JONES HAS OTHER CHILDREN IS IRRELEVANT, YOUR HONOUR!"'

'SUSPENSEFUL PAUSE. "SUSTAINED."

'I JUST FEEL SO OVERWHELMED SOMETIMES, IT'S IMPOSSIBLE FOR ME
TO KEEP AN EYE ON ALL OF THEM ALL OF THE TIME UNLESS I LOCK
THEM IN THE SAME ROOM.'

Statistics show that accidental death and serious injury rates during childhood have decreased significantly over the previous couple of decades. The wide-scale implementation of preventative safety measures has gone a long way to achieving its objective. Childproof caps on medicine bottles, pool fencing, seatbelts, baby capsules and numerous public-safety campaigns are a few examples of the successful drive to create a safer environment for children.

Unfortunately, the resulting fear of responsibility and litigation has conspired to create an environment that is also sterile and limited and in which the loss of a child leads not just to pain and grief but also to guilt and blame. We seem to have lost sight of the fact that despite prevention and vigilance, accidents will still happen.

LOSS

Last year, the youngest child of close friends of my husband's family drowned in the backyard swimming pool. A loss like this creates ripples of pain and grief that spread outwards from the unimaginable pain of the family at the centre. Alongside the outpouring of sympathy and compassion, a nasty symptom of our current age reared its head.

'The beauty of the world has two edges: one of laughter, one of anguish cutting the heart asunder.'

VIRGINIA WOOLF

People who had no business asking wanted to know the exact details of the tragedy. It wasn't just simple curiosity, many of those people were looking for someone to blame. Having someone to blame goes a long way to soothing our own fears, because if an accident is just an accident, then we too are vulnerable. If, on the other hand, we can somehow prove that someone is to blame for what happened, we can reassure ourselves that it will never happen to us, we would never be that stupid, careless or negligent. So the family did what all good families do, they closed ranks, kept their counsel and protected their remaining loved ones from the court of the gossips.

The grieving mother explained, 'I strived to be the perfect mother and I still lost a child. I have three children, two living and one in heaven.'

The death of a child is, thankfully, something that will remain outside the realm of experience for most of us. Even serious injury and illness are relatively rare, yet the fear that it could happen drives us as parents to consciously protect our offspring. The motivation that drives schools, councils, corporations and other organisations is a different kind of fear altogether – the fear of litigation. It's no bad thing to keep these bodies on their toes; it introduces a measure of responsibility for safety into a world that operates under the assumption 'caveat emptor' – let the buyer beware.

Safety standards have become something that all providers of goods and services are required to take very seriously. Why is it that every move towards improvement seems to lead to an endpoint of ridiculous overkill? Schools can no longer take any kind of action without considering Occuptional Health and Safety laws. The result? When the local school drew up a uniform guideline they excluded sandals for not meeting OHS standards. Sandals? I live in Australia, the land of the thong ('flip-flops' to non-Australians), yet my children are banned from wearing sandals, even on days when the mercury soars, because they might stub their toes. Enough! It's like there's a room somewhere full of people who have been employed to make things safe and now that they've run out of exciting problems, they have nothing to do, so they've turned their attention to every aspect of our lives.

'SCHOOLS ARE RUN AND MAINTAINED ON A TENDER SYSTEM; WHOEVER DOES IT CHEAPEST, GETS THE JOB. I WON'T EVEN START ON THE IDEOLOGICAL MADNESS OF THIS, BUT LET ME GIVE YOU AN EXAMPLE OF BUREAUCRACY COLLIDING WITH OHS. THE PRESCHOOL I TEACH IN WAS PROVIDED WITH TWO HEATERS, ONE OF WHICH NEVER WORKED, BY THE GOVERNMENT-APPROVED SUPPLIER. THE CLASSROOMS ARE OLD DEMOUNTABLES AND THEY ARE COLD AND DRAUGHTY; IN WINTER THOSE HEATERS ARE A NECESSITY.

'THE SUPPLIER CAME AND TOOK THE HEATER, COULDN'T GET THE PARTS, LOST THE TENDER TO ANOTHER COMPANY, PASSED THEM

AROUND, STILL NO PARTS, WINTER CAME AND 20 KIDS WERE LITERALLY FREEZING. WE HAD KIDS SICK EVERY WEEK; THOSE WITH ASTHMA GOT WORSE, PARENTS WERE OFFERING TO BRING IN HEATERS FROM HOME, BUT WE HAD TO SAY NO. EVEN IF THE HEATER WAS THE SAME KIND, EVEN THE SAME MODEL, AS THE ORIGINAL, SAFETY LAWS FORBID US TO USE ONE BROUGHT IN FROM OUTSIDE. SO THOSE POOR KIDS FROZE ALL WINTER IN THE NAME OF SAFETY.'

NEGOTIATING RISK

Conflict over levels of appropriate risk can be an ongoing bone of contention within families. My husband loves risk, thrives on it, longs for it. Cliff jumping? Tick. Parachuting? Tick. Riding a motorbike? Tick. That's right, all things he did and loved in the days before babies and he didn't give them up without a fight. He'd go out and buy a motorbike tomorrow if it weren't for me. Whenever he brings it up I go for the low blow and hit him with, 'Well, if you want to risk your own life, that's fine. By the way, do you think it's appropriate for children to attend funerals?' It's not just that he is prepared to take more risks than I am, it's that he genuinely perceives risk differently, and that extends to our kids. He takes risks that I couldn't bear to, but I've had to learn that he has a right to. Not to risk their lives, but a right to trust his judgment as I trust mine.

He took the kids to the park on Saturday, the ball went flat, they needed a pump and Tom offered to run home and get it. 'Great,' said hubby, 'It's in the shed.' I was sitting on the front verandah reading the paper; Tom strolled in and got the pump, and my heart froze. It took every fibre in my being not to march him back to the park and confront my husband, but I knew that I couldn't. The fact that he had chosen to allow something that I wouldn't didn't make him wrong.

The scary thing about those little risks is not the minimal chance that something could go wrong, but the minimal chance that something catastrophic could go wrong. Children do get hit and killed by cars and you cannot undo that split second that heralds a lifelong loss, nor can you always prevent it. It's the belief that you can stop it happening that stops you from giving them the freedom to grow up.

When I fly with my children, part of me believes I can keep that plane in the sky and my family safe through sheer force of will. The fact that my belief is patently ridiculous has no effect on my faith in it. I believe that if I escort my children at all times, they will remain safe; my husband believes that it's safe to allow our son to walk home on his own. We are both wrong – there are no guarantees either way.

'My friends' little boy was hit and killed crossing the road,' says Felicity. 'They were going to play with the neighbours; she was holding hands with both of her sons. In a split second, the younger boy, impatient to get there, pulled his hand from hers and darted across the road. He was hit and died instantly and even though she was there, she was powerless to stop it happening. To make it even worse, the man who was driving the car had lost a daughter in the same way. Now he had to deal with his loss and inflicting the same pain on another family, even though he was completely blameless, just in the wrong place at the wrong time.'

Received wisdom would have it that men are always the risk-takers and women the cautious ones. More than that, society demands that women accept that role for themselves. Several years ago, a British mountain climber, who also happened to be the mother of young children, perished while climbing. Media coverage made it clear that she had betrayed her children, the nation and the very state of motherhood. She was forever a mother-of-two, who dared to follow a dream and callously left them motherless. When fathers die in the pursuit of personal goals, it's a tragedy; when mothers do the same, it's a betrayal.

'MY HUSBAND AND I JUST CANNOT AGREE ON HOW MUCH INDEPENDENCE ALICE IS ENTITLED TO. WE ALMOST CAME TO BLOWS OVER IT ONE WEEKEND BECAUSE WE WERE SO ENRAGED BY THE OTHER'S PERCEIVED STUPIDITY. I LET ALICE GO NEXT DOOR TO PLAY WITH JAMIE. JAMIE'S MUM POPPED HER HEAD IN TO SAY SHE WAS GOING TO THE SHOPS, AND DID I WANT ANYTHING, AND WOULD I KEEP AN EAR OUT WHILE SHE WAS GONE.

'WHEN DAVID GOT HOME HE WANTED ALICE TO HELP PLANT A LITTLE TREE HE'D BOUGHT. I DIRECTED HIM NEXT DOOR AND HE CAME BACK WITH BOTH KIDS AND A THUNDEROUS LOOK ON HIS FACE. HE SENT THE KIDS OUTSIDE TO LOOK FOR A GOOD SPOT AND THEN JUST LET RIP, TELLING ME I WAS IRRESPONSIBLE AND STUPID AND NOT TO BE TRUSTED.

'I WAS FURIOUS AND DEMANDED TO KNOW WHEN SHE WOULD BE OLD ENOUGH. HE JUST SAID, "NEVER!" AND STORMED OUT. THAT'S THE THING THAT PISSES ME OFF, NOT THAT HE DISAGREES WITH ME, BUT THAT HE WON'T EVEN THINK IT THROUGH REASONABLY.'

While we argue over appropriate levels of risk and agonise over the trade-off between safety and freedom, our children are becoming the hidden generation. A grandmother was overheard asking at the local park, 'Where are all the children?'. We've become our own worst enemies, by keeping our children off the streets we have helped ensure that the streets are not a safe place for them to be. For a start, there is safety in numbers. When we were out playing as kids, we were playing together or, at the very least, side by side. The big kids looked out for the littlies and, as you grew, you in turn looked after those coming up behind you. When kids were out on the streets, they were by definition part of the community. People knew they were there and kept an eye on them.

We clear our children off the streets because we are worried about cars, then we put them into cars and add to the problem. By taking them off the streets we have given drivers free rein. Cars didn't race along the street I grew up on and it was partly because there was a very good chance they would plough straight into a game of cricket if they did. Remove children from the street and you remove the need for drivers to watch out for them. Remove children from their community and you remove that community's duty of care for their young. Ghettoise children and you will leave them a legacy of alienation and isolation. Reclaim your streets, reclaim your parks; our children have the same right to roam that we did and we should not allow that to be taken away.

'It takes a village to raise a child.'

AFRICAN PROVERB

'IN THE END IT'S NOT THE YEARS
IN YOUR LIFE THAT COUNT, IT'S
THE LIFE IN YOUR YEARS.'

ABRAHAM LINCOLN

Picture of health

'Happiness is nothing more than good health and a
bad memory.'

ALBERT SCHWEITZER

While you are still pregnant, the subtle and constant fears of parents are a mystery to you. Watching someone worry about their toddler's hearing or their daughter's propensity to chubbiness can be perplexing. While you're still carrying the fear of life-threatening congenital diseases, the vagaries of childhood health can easily appear trivial. Until, that is, you've delivered the perfectly healthy newborn you were statistically likely to give birth to. Then you're in for a crash course in the anxious life of the worried well. Which is not be be dismissive; scarlet fever, polio, tuberculosis and all the other diseases that used to strike fear into every parent's heart no longer sweep through childhood like an indiscriminate broom. Yet children still get sick, struggle with various syndromes and sometimes die and we as their parents are charged with coping with all of it, from the difficult to the unimaginable. What I didn't anticipate was that I would end up being responsible for the health of the entire family. Sometimes I feel like Matron, doling out paracetamol to feverish children, ice-packs to an injured husband and bandaids for an injured visitor. Compounding the initial shock was the horror of discovering how often my kids were destined to either be ill or require some kind of medical attention. At one stage I was beginning to feel as though I had given birth to a bunch of sickly weaklings. In the UK you cannot plan a picnic for fear of the rain, in my kingdom you must always have a contingency plan in case of illness. Mum unwittingly made it worse when she mused on the continual ill-health of my children, finishing off by saying, 'I'm sure you and your brothers and sisters weren't sick so often'. The very next day I read in the paper that the average preschool child is sick eight times each year. Bingo, I thought, we've got three, and eight times three is 24! Praise the Lord, we are normal. My doctor confirmed my diagnosis. 'Francesca,' he said, 'It happens all the time. When families are young I see more of the mother and the kids than most grandparents. For some families my waiting room becomes a home away from home. Then one day, I realise I haven't seen them for a while and I'll wonder whether they've moved out of the neighbourhood. Occasionally that's the case, but usually it's just that they've grown up. As kids get older their immune systems develop and they don't get sick as often as they used to. The families who keep on coming are the ones who have a child with asthma or allergies.'

THE UNHEALTHY GENERATION?

Cleanliness is next to godliness so it follows that dirt is evil. Rising standards of cleanliness combined with smaller families have seen infection rates fall across the developed world. At the same time we've seen a concurrent rise in the rates of asthma and allergies. While fewer families will have to deal with serious illness or death, there has been a massive upsurge in chronic conditions that require constant daily management. For the past few decades, science has searched for a solution to the asthma conundrum. Why is it that while most health outcomes are getting better these 'diseases of affluence' are on the increase?

'I'M AT A LOSS TO UNDERSTAND WHERE JACK'S ASTHMA COMES FROM. NEITHER OF US SMOKES AND NEVER HAS. WE BOTH EAT WELL AND EXERCISE REGULARLY. I WAS ESPECIALLY CAREFUL DURING MY PREGNANCY AND WHILE I WAS BREASTFEEDING, WHICH I DID FOR THE WHOLE FIRST YEAR. THE FIRST TIME I FOUND HIM GASPING FOR BREATH IN HIS COT I THOUGHT I WAS GOING TO PASS OUT. WE'RE OVER THE SHOCK NOW AND HAVE LEARNED TO CONTROL IT, BUT THE FEAR THAT HE MIGHT HAVE AN ATTACK THAT KILLS HIM NEVER GOES AWAY. SOMETIMES I THINK, "I FOLLOWED ALL THE RULES, SO WHY US, WHY JACK?".'

As a layman, it's hard to understand where all of these sick kids come from. Looking back, there was one girl in my year with asthma and basically no one with an allergy, at least not a life-threatening one. There were no epi-pens, no school-wide bans on peanut butter, just the odd kid who thought claiming ownership of a pea allergy was a smart way to get out of eating his vegies. It's clear that over the past decade or so there has been a dramatic increase in the number of children with life-threatening allergies, particularly to peanuts and shellfish. If you've ever seen someone suffer from anaphylactic shock you'll know that there is nothing amusing or trivial about it. It is swift and deadly without appropriate treatment. It's also way outside the scope of what most of us will have to deal with. What is more pervasive, and harder to get a handle on, is the number of children with food intolerances. Last year in my daughter's preschool class there were six children out of 20, that's 30 per cent of the class, who had 'red letter' eating plans pinned to the wall of the class. Some of these three-year-olds were confined to diets so unpleasant and restrictive that food must seem more like a punishment than a pleasure or a basic necessity of life.

So where did all these delicate kids come from? Why does it appear we have given life to such a fragile and unhealthy generation? I'm going to go out on a limb here, and probably earn myself plenty of hate mail, and say that we haven't. It's not that our children are weaker than we were, but that we see the whole area of health through an entirely different prism. Health is no longer just about medicine, about treating the unwell; it's about optimisation. We live in an incredibly solution-driven era, a time when we are no longer prepared to accept that Johnny is just a 'sickly child' without searching for answers and, preferably, a cure. We have also created a culture that is infinitely more aware of the complexities of health and therefore more willing to diagnose conditions that were unheard of even a few decades ago. On top of this, we have, as a society, continually stretched the borders of a variety of conditions so that many of us who would have fallen outside the net are now caught within it.

The structure of our medical system means that doctors are also more willing to give a child with problems a label as it makes it easier for the parents to gain access to the therapies that would benefit their child. Put these same children within the confines of an educational curriculum that measures their abilities to a microscopic degree and what you end up with is a generational conundrum – how can it be that these kids have access to the best medicine available and yet such a depressing statistical outlook? How do we reconcile the fact that our children have inherited the longest life expectancy in history with the fact that so many of them are ostensibly unwell? It seems inescapable that part of the problem is our current willingness to leap for a label that defines the problems we might be struggling with. Not achieving at school? Time to search for a learning difficulty. Clumsy? Must be dyspraxia. Finds it hard to make friends? Maybe I should have him assessed for Asperger's syndrome.

Rather than accepting our children the way they are, we feel compelled to reach for every available tool to enhance their potential and release the real person inside. I'm not saying this is a bad thing, on the contrary, I can look back through my Year 5 class and see several children who would have benefited from more therapy and less discipline. What I am saying is that in our rush to do our best for our children, we need to make sure we are not making things worse.

THE VALUE OF INSTINCT

'ONE OF MY SONS IS REALLY CLUMSY,' SAYS SALLY. HE JUST FALLS OVER ALL THE TIME, RUNS INTO THINGS AND BANGS HIS HEAD. I'D NEVER REALLY WORRIED ABOUT IT, JUST THOUGHT IT WAS PART OF WHO HE WAS, AND I GUESS THE FACT THAT MY BROTHER WAS SIMILAR AT HIS AGE MADE IT SEEM NATURAL TO ME. I DIDN'T GIVE IT MUCH THOUGHT UNTIL HIS YEAR 4 TEACHER MADE A BIG DEAL ABOUT IT. SHE GAVE US A LIST OF POSSIBLE SYNDROMES AND SUGGESTED WE TAKE HIM TO OUR GP FOR REFERRAL TO A SPECIALIST. MY GP SPENT SOME TIME CHATTING TO MY SON, GOT HIM TO DO A COUPLE OF TASKS FOR HIM AND THEN SENT HIM OUT TO THE WAITING ROOM. HE SAID TO ME, "SALLY, I CAN SEND HIM TO AN OCCUPATIONAL THERAPIST IF YOU LIKE, BUT PERSONALLY I DON'T THINK THERE IS ANYTHING WRONG WITH HIM. I KNOW YOU'RE UNDER A LOT OF PRESSURE, BUT MY BEST

GUESS WOULD BE THAT SAM WILL JUST GROW INTO HIS BODY AND OUT OF HIS AWKWARDNESS." I WAS TOTALLY RELIEVED TO HAVE SOMEONE BACK UP MY INSTINCT AS A MOTHER AND HAVE NEVER REGRETTED LEAVING WELL ALONE.'

The most important aspect of Sally's experience, for her, was the relief she felt when her doctor validated her instinct.

'I JUST COULDN'T SEE HOW PUTTING HIM THROUGH THE STRESS OF ASSESSMENTS AND PROGRAMS WOULD HELP HIM IN THE LONG TERM. IT WASN'T AS THOUGH HE WAS UNHAPPY WITH THE WAY HE WAS, SO WHY FOCUS ON IT? IN THE END, HE DID GROW OUT OF IT AND I'M GLAD WE DIDN'T WASTE OUR TIME AND MONEY ON THERAPY SESSIONS. INSTEAD, WE JUST SPENT EXTRA TIME OUTDOORS HAVING FUN TOGETHER.'

We are the generation of parents who have seen every episode of 'ER', have access to the internet and read every article on children and health. There's a vast gulf between fear and instinct and it's important we learn, as parents, to separate the two. Most of us would toss prescription medicines straight in the bin if we thought for a moment that the list of side-effects was actually going to apply to us. I haven't had a script with less than 20 possible, and serious, side-effects in the last ten years, yet I know that the chances of them applying to me are slim, and if they do, I am forewarned and forearmed. Give me a list of symptoms, however, and my reaction is the complete opposite. I can't read an article or stumble across a disease on the internet without immediately diagnosing either myself or one of my loved ones as a probable sufferer.

Being one of the worried well does not necessarily make me a better mother. Children do, and will, suffer from a variety of conditions and there are wonderful therapies available. The scary thing is when these conditions degenerate into the realms of a fad and the therapies that go with them are used to improve children who are just a little too normal for their parents. In my experience, when something really is wrong with your child, you are aware of it, and the guesswork is reserved for the doctors as they work towards a diagnosis.

Mothers often have an incredibly strong instinct when it comes to the health and wellbeing of their children. My doctor, with whom I have a very good relationship, says, 'Any good doctor needs to listen to the mother; no one knows the child as well as the mother.' Serious problems can arise when the medical profession dismisses the mother's instinct that something is wrong.

'When Amelia was born I knew straightaway that something wasn't right,' says Jane. 'I'd already had one child, Jake, and he'd been completely healthy. It wasn't that there was one obvious thing wrong with Amelia, it was more that it just didn't feel right. I told the doctors I was worried but they just sort of brushed me off. We went home after three days but only lasted two days at home. Amelia couldn't feed, she wasn't thriving and was losing weight at an alarming rate. They took us into hospital for a couple of days, then sent us home again. By this stage, all my alarm bells were ringing and after two more horrendous days at home, I took her back and said, "We're not leaving until you tell me what's wrong with my baby". That got their attention, besides which, it was obvious by then that there was definitely something wrong.'

Being unable to put a label on Amelia's problems made it difficult for the doctors to give Jane and her husband, Mark, an accurate diagnosis or an indication of what Amelia's outcome might be. 'By this stage, they were starting to say that Amelia essentially wouldn't have a future, that she would never be able to walk, talk or relate to us. They suggested that we begin thinking about a long-term-care situation. It was like the initial situation, but reversed. While I was glad they were taking things so seriously, the idea that there was no hope for Amelia just didn't ring true.'

In the end, Amelia spent nine months in hospital before Jane and Mark brought her home. 'It was hard bringing her home,' says Jane. 'We were living in an area with limited services and I was also acutely conscious of Jake and of the changes it would make to his life. In the end, we moved to an area with better provisions and I suppose I made it my goal to do my best for Amelia without depriving Jake of a normal childhood.' Following her instinct turned out to be the best thing Jane could have done. 'Amelia is definitely behind other kids her age, but she can walk, she's learning to talk better everyday, she goes to the local Montessori school and is on track to move to primary,' says Jane. If I'd listened to the doctors we would have been committing her to a life of institutions; we would have been betraying her.'

Looking back, one thing that strikes Jane is that she and Mark managed to keep their marriage intact throughout. 'When we'd go and spend time with Amelia at the hospital, we were in the minority, in fact, we were almost an oddity, being a family still together. So many of the children in the ward had separated parents and it was always the mother left to cope with the problems. I consider us blessed to have found a way to give Amelia a life without losing each other.'

'It is easy when we are in prosperity to give advice to the afflicted.'

AESCHYLUS

THE IMPACT OF A CHILD'S ILL HEALTH

It's not unusual for marriages to break up under the strain of dealing with a seriously ill child. When you think about the pressure child-rearing in general puts on the average relationship, it's easy to see how fragile bonds can shatter under the stress. 'Jeff and I had separated after our second girl was born, then we reconciled and I got pregnant again,' says Elise. 'Jeff wasn't happy that I was pregnant and then at the 20-week scan, they said there was a marker that could indicate Down syndrome and I should have an amniocentesis. Even before the amnio, Jeff wanted me to abort, but I couldn't. They gave me an all-clear after the test, but things were already really bad between Jeff and me.

'When Rosie was born, I said, "Has she got all her fingers and toes?" but nobody heard me,' says Elise. 'She was blue, they revived her, she went blue again and then again. In the end, they raced her off to the ICU and I was left alone in the labour ward for an hour. I had a shower and sobbed my heart out, then they brought her to me in a humidicrib for me to say goodbye before they transferred her to another hospital.' Rosie was eventually diagnosed with VATER syndrome and Elise was faced with managing a baby who had an ongoing list of serious health problems.

'She's had operations on her oesophagus, her bowel and bladder, and kidney problems and a hole in the heart. I deal with it all on my own. Jeff is a decent father to the girls, but we are definitely separated and he basically leaves me to deal with all of the problems related to Rosie's health. At one stage he actually accused me of having had an affair, saying he didn't believe Rosie was his. If there had been any chance of us reconciling, dealing with Rosie's problems put an end to that.' Obviously there are plenty of committed fathers who wouldn't dream of abdicating the care of their children, well or not, but caring for the ill has traditionally been seen as women's work and women are often still left to do more than their fair share.

'Phil is great when it comes to the children's health. When they were younger he'd willingly do his share of night-time comforting and now that they've grown up he's really serious about helping them live healthy lives. He takes them swimming, bike riding, down to the park for a kick around. He makes sure they eat well and have a good understanding of how to respect their bodies. I just wish he'd take the same attitude when it comes to his health. While he does all the right things with food and exercise, he refuses to admit it when he's sick and never, ever goes to the doctor. Sometimes I worry that if something does go seriously wrong, by the time he does get help it will be too late.'

MEN'S HEALTH/THE WEEKEND WARRIOR

Men are notorious for taking a head-in-the-sand approach to their health. Whether you consult statistics or a gaggle of wives, you'll find the same result – men regularly endanger their wellbeing by refusing to visit the doctor. Once or twice a year the newspapers will run a story on the difference in life expectancy and health outcomes between men and women. Invariably the story will provoke a letter to the editor that runs something like this:

'WHAT'S THE DEAL WITH WOMEN'S LIBERATION WHEN MEN ARE DYING YOUNG! WHERE ARE THE MEN'S GROUPS DEMANDING SOMETHING BE DONE! WOMEN HAVE HAD IT ALL THEIR OWN WAY FOR TOO LONG! SOMETHING MUST BE DONE!'

Fantastic, isn't it, the way that some people can make everything our fault? I always want to take the writer of these vicious little letters by the shoulders, give him a good shake and advise him to get over it. For a start, it's so divisive, the idea that doing something for one group negates helping another. Secondly, and listen carefully here, Mr Missive, women live longer in part because they take responsibility for their own health. In essence, our letter-writing friend is demanding that we also take responsibility for our husbands' health.

In my personal circle, many families are suffering from the phenomenon of the weekend warrior. Hubby spends all week hunched behind a desk, slobbing on the sofa watching TV and lounging in the bath. Come Sunday afternoon he strides out onto the field, a god in his own mind, to do battle over the ball. Broken toes, pulled muscles, damaged backs and cracked heads ensue, putting Daddy out of action for the next couple of days. Luckily for him, he usually regains peak form just in time for the next game, thereby completing the cycle.

Some weeks ago I dropped off my husband's phone at his office. A man hobbled into the lift on crutches. 'Let me guess,' said I, 'Soccer?'

'Yes' he replied, wincing, as he tried to manoeuvre through the doors.

'My husband, too, busted his foot playing on Sunday.'

He said, 'Be gentle with him.' The look he gave me, on the other hand, said, 'Please be kind; I know your sympathy bank is in the red, that this probably isn't the first time he's hobbled home, and it won't be the last, but it matters to him, that hour and a half on a Sunday afternoon when he doesn't have a job, or kids, or even a wife; it's just him and the blokes and the ball and the cheering crowd of his dreams.'

My look was equally eloquent. 'I know he loves it; it makes him feel young, feel fit, feel like the boy he once was and the man he thought he would be. It's not that I don't want him to play just because he's nearly 40, more that I want him to play as though he's nearly 40.'

'JOE HURT HIS BACK PLAYING FOOTY ON THE WEEKEND. HE HOBBLED HOME BENT DOUBLE AND GROUCHED ON THE SOFA WITH A COLD PACK AND A BEER. IT WAS BAD ENOUGH FOR HIM TO TAKE MONDAY OFF, WHICH IS ALMOST UNHEARD OF, AND EVEN THOUGH IT GOT MOSTLY BETTER, THE PAIN WOULDN'T FULLY GO AWAY. I KEPT ON AT HIM TO GO TO THE PHYSIO, BUT HE JUST WOULDN'T DO IT. HIS BACK GOT WORSE AND WORSE AND FINALLY I PUT MY FOOT DOWN – NO PHYSIO, NO SEX, NOT THAT HE WAS REALLY CAPABLE OF PERFORMING ANYWAY. FINALLY HE GOES, AND COMES HOME WITH A LIST OF EXERCISES, SIX FOLLOW-UP BOOKINGS ALREADY MADE AND A LIST OF TOYS HE NEEDED TO BUY TO STRENGTHEN HIS BACK. IT ENDED UP COSTING US A FORTUNE, WAY MORE THAN IF HE'D GONE STRAIGHTAWAY.'

'Age is something that doesn't matter, unless you are a cheese.'

BILLIE BURKE

Refusing to take matters of health seriously can extend beyond the physical arena. Mental illness is an area in which, statistically, more women seek treatment while men make up the greater percentage of sufferers. From depression to bipolar to schizophrenia, men are more likely to draw the short straw and so it follows that our sons as they move to manhood are equally at risk. It's a white-knuckle ride giving birth to a boy-child. Read the short guide to almost any condition outside breast cancer and hip-dysplasia and you'll find a line that reads, 'More common in boys than girls', or 'More likely to affect men than women'. Boys are more likely to die in infancy, childhood, the teenage years, young adulthood and adulthood. Assuming you get them through the early years, you're faced with the spectre of pranks gone wrong, cars driven wildly and mental illness and suicide.

It's hardly surprising if parents feel helpless in the face of statistics, but there is one very important thing we, as mothers, can do now to make a difference: teach our sons, as well as our daughters, to respect and cherish their bodies and their minds and to take responsibility for maintaining them.

TAKING CARE OF YOU

Right, exhausted yet? I thought so, which is a bit of a shame, really, because there is one more member of the family relying on you to look after them: you. You see, somewhere along the line you have to find time to look after yourself. Five serves of vegetables, three of fruit, plenty of calcium and a brisk daily walk are the supporting arms of my intended lifestyle. Lice, fleas and the flu (the kids, dogs and me, respectively) are too often my reality. When I'm sick I call my mother, hoping for words of comfort. I usually get them, but I'm also quizzed on what the doctor says and, 'For goodness sake, what do you mean you haven't been yet?'. Should I mention my aching back to my mother-in-law, I get sympathy wrapped up in incredulity; not going straight to the osteopath is not just beyond understanding, apparently it's wilful neglect. Woe betide yours truly should I complain to my sister-in-law about being tired and having a headache. Apparently it has nothing to do with pulling a late night at the computer, being woken twice before dawn and still having to get the tribe off to school. No, it's all down to not exercising. Why don't I just fit in a run? It's not that they don't care; they do, manifestly and passionately. It's just that they don't understand. I haven't been to the doctor because I haven't got time, I haven't been to the osteo because I haven't got time, and I haven't been for a run because I HAVEN'T GOT TIME!

'So,' they chorus, 'make time!' and I am left speechless and ashamed because they, of course, are right. I make time for just about everything else I have to do (Year 1 homework and nail-clipping sometimes slip off the end of the list) and even sometimes the things I want to do, so how do I justify neglecting the things I need to do? I don't, justify it, that is. I just ignore it and hope it will go away. I cancel my appointment with the osteopath because I'm juggling deadlines, homework and housework and I just can't finesse my schedule any more. So then my back goes completely and it's goodbye schedule, hello bed rest. Whenever I find myself bound to the bed by my own stupidity, I repent and shiver at the thought of what would happen if I were to be seriously unwell, incapacitated or even, God forbid, destined to die an early death? If my husband's efforts to keep house while I convalesce are anything to go by, it wouldn't be a pretty sight.

All flippancy aside, it's somehow only when I'm unavailable to my family that I am able to acknowledge the true value of the role I play within it. Losing Mummy would leave a huge void at the heart of my family, and of yours. It's worth reminding yourself once in a while that just because you're a hypochondriac doesn't mean it's not cancer. There are certain things you owe yourself and your family. Eat well, live well and (believe me, I know this is a toughie for some of us) don't smoke. Drink in moderation, check your breasts and above all, listen to your body. If it's telling you something you don't like the sound of, listen and act. When it comes to your health, practise what you preach and care for yourself like you do for your loved ones; none of them can do it for you.

'WHEN THEY FOUND OUT MY STEPFATHER WAS DYING, HE AND MY MOTHER DECIDED TO BE REALLY OPEN ABOUT IT WITH ME AND MY SISTER. THEY TOLD US CLEARLY THAT HE HAD VERY LITTLE TIME LEFT AND BETWEEN US WE DREW UP A LIST OF ALL THE THINGS WE COULD DO BEFORE HE DIED. WE DIVIDED IT INTO 'WANTS, NEEDS AND SHOULDS', THEN WE DREW A BIG CROSS THROUGH THE SHOULDS AND CONCENTRATED ON THE REST. IT MADE OUR TIME TOGETHER SPECIAL, BUT IT DIDN'T MAKE HIS DEATH ANY EASIER FOR US.'

Death is a possibility for all of us, but there's not a high probability it will happen right now. Breaking down due to neglect and overwork is a much more likely scenario. One thing I have never regretted is finally listening to my female relatives and getting serious about maintenance. I now like to think of my body as a car. Not, unfortunately, a sleek, flashy sports car, more a comfortable but well-maintained all-wheel drive. In the end, Mum was right: use the right fuel, visit the mechanic and make sure you open it up on the freeway from time to time and it will keep running smoothly.

'If my doctor told me I had six months to live, I wouldn't brood. I'd type a little faster.'

ISAAC ASIMOV

'CHILDHOOD: THE PERIOD
OF HUMAN LIFE INTERMEDIATE
BETWEEN THE IDIOCY OF
INFANCY AND THE FOLLY OF
YOUTH – TWO REMOVES FROM
THE SIN OF MANHOOD
AND THREE FROM THE
REMORSE OF AGE.'

AMBROSE BIERCE

Too cool for school

'Education is the most powerful weapon you can use to change the world.'

NELSON MANDELA

After the jaw-dropping expense of childcare (one year I actually spent almost my entire after-tax income paying other people to act in loco parentis), starting real school comes as a massive financial relief. Big school is a big deal in any child's life. It's an even bigger deal in the parents' life. It's a cliché, one that has been mercilessly exploited by advertisers, but the first time you see your child in a real school uniform you know you're at the start of another big adventure. What no one tells you beforehand is how much of an adventure it will be for you. They also decline to mention, in case it scares you off, just how much work it will be for you. All you have to do in order to appreciate the demands placed on parents of school-age children is check two remarkably different places – the front gate of the school and the letters page of the newspaper. It's no secret that parents are locked into a school run that didn't even exist 20 years ago. Parents are blithely demonised for having the gall to run their children to and from school; apparently we're making them fat, depriving them of the opportunity to learn to walk the streets on their own, clogging up the roads instead of leaving them free for the busy tradesmen and commuters who need them so much more than us, and are single-handedly responsible for the surge in the sales of grunt-laden four-wheel drives and the concurrent upswing in accident statistics.

I sometimes wonder if anyone's thought to bring the predators of the jungle of opinion somewhat up to date. For a start, there's the element of choice – that is, those who rail against us seem to assume that we automatically have one. It may be a petty point, but the parents of littlies, that is preschool, kindergarten and Year 1 children, are required to drop them off and pick them up. Even after the days of sign-in and out are over, children are escorted outside by their teachers and forbidden to leave until their parent/carer/neighbour has been sighted and identified. Now, in the best of all possible worlds, we would all, obviously, walk our children to and from school to keep them fit and spend some quality time quietly chatting about their stimulating day at school. Unfortunately, that precludes Mum from working full time and fails to take into account the vagaries of other siblings, either younger or already at different schools, after-school activities that start a bare 15 minutes after the bell has gone and all the other random elements that conspire to make my day, at least, as unpredictable as possible. So most of us have barely got the kids off to school and already we've run the gauntlet of public opinion, personal guilt and political blindness and it only gets thornier as the day goes on. If you're just starting out on the great adventure of school, my advice is to grow a thick hide in double-quick time, or resign yourself to 13 years of martyrdom.

Back in the good old days when I was busy navigating the wilds of the blackboard jungle, my mother was essentially released to get on with her day. I clearly remember her walking me there on my first day – I got a nosebleed halfway there and bled profusely on my long-anticipated uniform – but after that, it was up to me. There was no signing in and signing out, no listening to reading in the classroom, no mummies waiting at the gate, just a heaving pack of kids jumping onto bikes and heading off to vandalise the local shopping centre. Now most kids have a schedule that rivals the Queen's and require an escort at all times. Unfortunately for us, we can either buckle down and accept it, or lobby to change the way that society operates. Your choice is your own, and if you're going for option two, you have my whole-hearted support, but don't go into it unless you're prepared for a long, hard slog. Arrayed against you are the Department of Education and the arbiters of public opinion, and together they're a scary team.

STARTING SCHOOL

Starting big school was a bit of a shock for me, there was this sudden, and precipitous, loss of influence accompanied by a massive increase in responsibility. My eldest was lucky to score one of the best kindergarten teachers ever put on this earth, and for the first few days she seemed happy for me to wander into the class, have a nose around and a chat, just like I had at preschool. By day three, I felt this unfamiliar pressure to leave her to it, and by the end of the week, she was all but standing at the door and keeping the parents out like the most unbending of bouncers. It wasn't just me either, all of us neophytes with one precious kid starting kindy found ourselves drifting aimlessly outside the school, unwilling to admit that we'd been effectively barred and unsure what to do about it. Of course, now I'm older and wiser I realise that the teachers were doing exactly what was needed, swiftly educating us ignorant parents in the ways of the big world, and making it clear that, from now on, between the hours of nine and three, our kids had to fend for themselves. Once the realisation had sunk in, we parents took it with varying degrees of grace, but take it we did because, for the first time, we had no say in the matter.

Personally I felt guiltily relieved to be effectively banned from the classroom, with two younger kids and a full-time job, I felt like I'd been given an out-clause. Besides, it became swiftly evident that one's level of involvement was a matter of personal choice, and those who were making it their business to do whatever they could were making it possible for me to do what I needed to do. The point of barring parents at the door of the kindy class was ultimately not to keep parents out of the class. At the end of the day, the demands of the curriculum mean that teachers can't do it without help from parents. The point, in fact, was to cut the apron strings and force us to let our children go, to make us let them make their own way through the school day.

But just because you have to leave them to it doesn't mean they can actually do it on their own. Your role becomes that of a coach, giving everything you can to help them off the field so that they can run the best race possible. That means helping with homework, running an activity schedule that would make a government minister's aide wince and somehow managing to be a better person than you really are. You see, for most kids it's not the stuff that happens in the classroom that makes school tough, but the stuff that happens outside it.

COMPETITION BEGINS EARLY

Tina learnt the hard way that when it comes to kids and their parents, the tough stuff starts early. 'One thing I didn't anticipate when Tabby started school was the level of competition, and I don't mean between the kids but between the parents. At the beginning of Year 4 the school announced that they would be running a 4/5 composite class as they didn't have the numbers for two straight classes. I didn't think twice about which class Tabs would be in until the playground rumours started. It was like everyone suddenly went mad, assuming that composite must mean selective. Year 4 parents were feeling smug if their kids were in 4/5, one dad actually said to me, "I'm just so surprised Gabby made it into 4/5, I didn't think she was that academic".

'It didn't start to bother me until it began causing friction between Tabby and her buddy Jules. Jules started boasting that being in the composite meant she'd skipped Year 4 and was much smarter than Tabs. When Tabby had a little cry about it at bedtime I found out that all the kids were talking about it in the playground, which made me see red as that kind of thing comes from one place, and that's home.

'In the end, a couple of other parents and I agitated for the school to set the record straight in the newsletter, we just mentioned the magic word "bullying" and the principal devoted a whole page to explaining the situation and firmly squashing the rumours of academic selection. I have to admit, though, much as I loathe the smug and competitive, I did get a little frisson of victory when I discovered a few weeks later that Tabby was scoring levels ahead of her "smarter" friend. I celebrated with a few glasses of white wine before vowing to nip my incipient smugness in the bud.'

'SPORT WAS WHERE COMPETITION REALLY GOT UGLY, NOT AMONG THE KIDS BUT AMONG THE PARENTS. THERE WAS ONE DAD IN PARTICULAR WHO WAS JUST OUT OF CONTROL. HE WAS PERFECTLY NICE 99 PER CENT OF THE TIME, BUT PUT HIS KID ON A SPORTING FIELD, IN A POOL, ANYWHERE COMPETITION WAS GOING ON, AND HE TURNED INTO A TOTAL NIGHTMARE. HE TRIED PRETTY HARD NOT TO SHOUT AND SCREAM AS THEY BAN YOU PRETTY QUICKLY IF YOU DO. INSTEAD, HE WAS ICY AND SARCASTIC AND, FRANKLY, PRETTY SCARY. IT GOT TO THE POINT WHERE JOE DIDN'T WANT TO BE ON THE TEAM ANY MORE.

'IN THE END, THE COACH BARRED HIM FROM ATTENDING TRAINING OR ANY GAMES UNTIL HE'D LEARNT TO CHANGE THE WAY HE DEALT WITH THE KIDS. YOU CAN'T GET AWAY FROM IT, THOUGH, THE VERY NEXT MATCH THERE WAS A PARENT FROM THE OTHER TEAM WHO WAS HISSING THREATS AT BOTH HIS OWN TEAM AND THE OPPOSITION. SCARY THING IS, I'M TALKING ABOUT EIGHT-YEAR-OLDS HERE!'

It's amazing the extent to which we're prepared to put our kids under the microscope at such a young age. There seems to be a clear split in the playground between those who monitor results from the beginning and those who just think school should be fun for the little ones.

In some ways, Year 1 can be the hardest for kids and parents alike. Kindy is a magical year where everything is new and, in many ways, your kids are still babies. If you're lucky, your school will run a buddy system and those worldly Year Sixers will take your little fledglings under their wings for the whole of the year. By comparison, Year 1 is a rude shock; they're in it on their own and this is when jockeying for position in the pecking order starts in earnest. Suddenly other people's children, and your own, come into focus like never before, and the picture isn't always pretty.

It's all so easy when they're little; essentially your children play with the children of adults who you like, and, as little children will, they play, squabble, laugh and bite fairly indiscriminately. While you may have to make the odd apology or strategically swift exit, most small children don't really have friends, just equally miniature diversions who allow their mothers to get on with the business of chatting and drinking coffee.

School friends, as anyone who has been at school will remember, are an entirely different kettle of fish. They are, in fact, the real deal, the first people outside your family who will have a definable and long-lasting effect on who you are and the way you feel about yourself. No wonder friends are generally more terrifying for parents than every other aspect of school put together.

As Annie tells it, 'Primary school, I used to tell anyone who'd listen, is not really about learning. So long as kids come out of school knowing how to read and write, the school has done its job. Primary school is really about socialisation, I used to say. School had been academically really difficult for me, but socially a breeze. I just assumed that it would be the same for Jack, and I guess I was preparing for Jack to be average in class but pretty popular. Well, you can guess what happened. Jack turned out to be incredibly smart and awkward, just like his dad, really, and I was the one who found it really hard.'

Unfortunately (or maybe not, for it's hard to draw the line at where we are needed and where our children are simply becoming ciphers for our own fears), there's very little you can do to change things when your beloved is on a sticky wicket in the playground. Not that I mean to say there is nothing you can do, of course there is, but that your powers are limited and that is not going to change. However, there's nothing like a bit of power judiciously used behind the scenes. 'When Louis started acting out at home I thought he was just being a pain in the bum,' relates Amelia. 'I was pretty busy at work and at home and, at first, I just got angry instead of paying attention. Then he started saying that he didn't want to go to school that day because his tummy hurt or his back hurt. It didn't take a genius to work out that something was bugging him at school.

Then I had one of those crap days that just happen; I was running late for everything at work and jumped in the car to go to a meeting. Then I saw Lou's lunchbox still sitting on the front seat. I had one of those "mad mummy moments" when you feel like the worst mother ever. I decided it didn't matter how late I was, I had to get Lou's lunch to him. Looking back, I could have just called the school and ordered lunch from the canteen, but it was only because I went there that I realised what was going on. Just as I jumped out of the car, the bell rang for recess and the playground just went mad. I got to Lou's class and popped the box in his bag and then went looking for him to give him his recess. I found him under the big tree at the back of the school. He was with the boys he always hangs out with, but one of them, Josh, had him in a headlock. I felt really sick and had to stop myself from dragging Josh off him. It's not as bad as it sounds, it's partly just the way boys play at that age, and they were all pretending to fight. But the rest of them were having fun, and I could see from Louis' face that he wasn't. He knew it was meant to be fun, but for him it was just scary.'

It can be hard to deal with the frailties of our children without being made to feel that we're fussing about nothing. 'I talked to my husband about it, but he just laughed and said, "Come on, Milly, it's called being a boy." But I still didn't think it was funny. In the end, I enrolled him in tae kwon do, and it made all the difference. It was like the rough stuff in the playground went from being something scary to something he could control.'

'MY ELDEST IS IN YEAR 6 AND HANGS OUT WITH THE SAME TWO GIRLS SHE BUDDIED UP WITH IN YEAR 1. THEY'RE ALL DOWN TO GO TO THE SAME HIGH SCHOOL NEXT YEAR AND WHILE I SHOULD BE FEELING GOOD ABOUT THAT, I'M ACTUALLY FEELING PRETTY WORRIED. SAM IS A GOOD KID, SHE'S POPULAR AND WORKS HARD, JOINS IN SPORT AND DOES ART. I'M REALLY PROUD OF HER, AND WANT TO TRUST HER, BUT I NO LONGER TRUST ALICE AND NATASHA. EARLIER THIS TERM THERE WAS AN INCIDENT AT THE SCHOOL WHERE A BOY IN THEIR YEAR ENDED UP GETTING HURT QUITE BADLY. IT SOUNDS PATHETIC, GIRLS HURTING BOYS, BUT YOU SHOULD SEE HOW THE GIRLS TOWER OVER THEM AT THIS AGE! SAM WAS ONLY ON THE PERIPHERY OF WHAT HAPPENED, BUT SHE STILL GOT A WARNING, THE FIRST TIME EVER! IT WORRIES ME TO THE POINT THAT I'VE BOOKED AN APPOINTMENT AT HER HIGH SCHOOL TO MAKE SURE THAT SHE, ALICE AND NATASHA ARE NOT IN THE SAME CLASS.'

DEALING WITH THE LOSS OF INNOCENCE

For parents, it's not always the big stuff in the playground that threatens the tranquillity of their little family. Bullying and learning difficulties are high on the agenda of most schools. There are programs in place to deal with them, and talking to your class teacher or principal is all it usually takes to get the ball rolling. Sometimes the really scary stuff is the subtle stuff, the incursion of worldly notions into the protected innocence of our children. It doesn't take long to realise that when they are in the playground, they are unlikely to be talking about maths and our kids are learning all kinds of things that we haven't got around to teaching them yet. That loss of innocence can mean anything from the truth about Santa to discovering the existence of pocket money, but should it get sticky it will usually be thanks to sex.

'It didn't take long for sex to become a big thing,' remembers Sarah. 'First of all, Ruby had a whole load of questions about sex. That was cool with me, but then she started talking about sex in this knowing way, and that was really freaky. I'd just cut the conversation short, but when she had her friends over I'd hear them talking about who was "sexing" whom and I have to admit, I just didn't know how to deal with it.'

When it comes to the younger years, dealing with it is usually just a matter of tolerance. Only in rare cases does it become something that requires adult intervention. 'Our local primary school had a really full-on situation,' tells Fiona, 'way beyond what usually goes on. Some of the Year 3 boys had this thing going where they'd go to the boys' toilets and they'd take it in turns for one of the boys to put his penis in another boy's mouth. It was a real scandal when the school found out about it and although none of the boys was thrown out, all kinds of programs were put into place and, of course, all the parents were talking about it. I felt kind of sorry for the boys involved; you've got to think that one of them has seen something he shouldn't have at that age, and brought it into the school with him.'

At least when your kids are really young the chances are you will find out what is going on and, hard as it might be, come up with a way to reassert control. Situations get even stickier in the later grades when kids have discovered that the code of *omerta* works as well for them as it does for the Mafia. Silence may be golden, but when it comes to running rings around teachers and parents alike, it is also the most potent weapon in the playground arsenal. Parents can be as complicit in the culture of secrecy as their children. It's so easy to empathise with the painful embarrassment of early pubescence that your instinct is often to continue the silence. Whether your kid is struggling with reading or ridicule it's easy to feel that making it public will make it worse. Consciously or not, by keeping quiet we are playing by the same rules that dominated us as kids, and playing right into the bullies' hands.

'AL WAS BIG FOR HIS AGE RIGHT FROM BIRTH, AND EVEN THOUGH HE WAS GENTLE, HE'D GET PULLED INTO ROUGH PLAY BY HIS OLDER BROTHERS. IT TURNED OUT TO BE A PROBLEM WHEN HE GOT INTO THE LATER GRADES AT SCHOOL. IF THERE WAS A FIGHT, AND HE WAS INVOLVED, HE'D ALWAYS END UP TAKING THE BLAME. I DIDN'T WANT HIM TO GET LABELLED, SO, AS I COULDN'T SUPERVISE HIM DURING SCHOOL HOURS, I ENROLLED HIM IN EVERY LUNCHTIME CLASS GOING, FROM CHESS TO CHOIR. HE KICKED AND SCREAMED ABOUT IT, ESPECIALLY WHEN I INSISTED HE DO THE DANCE CLASS. THE HYSTERICAL THING WAS HE ENDED UP LOVING DANCE AND STARTED DOING AN EXTRA CLASS ON THE WEEKENDS, BUT ONLY AFTER HE SWORE THE WHOLE FAMILY TO SECRECY.'

THE PRESSURE COOKER

It's not just the social stuff that hots up as the years fly past. The pressure of homework, exams and results hits giddy new altitudes as the spectre of high school looms ever closer. We've all read stories in the paper about kids as young as eight being tutored three or even four days a week on top of their everyday school work in the hope that they will pass the selective exams. Why? Call me old-fashioned, but if your kid can't get in without being hot-housed, what's the point of pushing them there? Surely you're just setting them up for six straight years of unbelievable pressure, as once they get there, the competition will be just as intense as the competition to get in in the first place. I haven't yet got that far down the schooling track, so maybe in a few years time I'll be forced to eat my words. But from where I stand now, I can't quite grasp the mania for testing and achievement at all costs that seems to have infiltrated the education system from day one.

When I look around me at the adults I know, I see people from all kinds of different backgrounds who followed incredibly different paths through life. They all ended up as fabulous people: interesting, informed, funny and fulfilled to varying degrees. So why is it that we're so afraid to allow our children the same freedom to forge their own path through life? When did we start to believe that all children should be ticking the same boxes and achieving the same results? That school could be and should be all things to all people? For that's exactly what children are – people, people who require nurturing and guidance, care and attention, but people nonetheless. So how can we expect our children to be something we are not ourselves? We can't, but that doesn't mean accepting them for who they are will be easy.

When my kids started school it catapulted me straight back through the decades. Logically I knew I was in my thirties, presentable and employable, but I still couldn't bring myself to call my son's teacher by her first name. If ever she called me over after school, my heart would race and I'd automatically start feeling guilty.

It made me realise that in some ways I'd never left school; the lessons I'd learnt there had lasted a lifetime. The tough thing was that this just heightened my reactions to my children's experiences of school. It's hard not to feel as though you are being assessed along with your children. Homework, uniforms and lunches can feel as much a reflection on you as something you do for your child. The problem is that you run the risk of making choices for your child based on how it makes you look rather than how it makes them feel.

The turning point for me was when son number two started preschool. My boys are basically pretty different souls and this was highlighted by the second having the same teacher as the first. I'd ask at the end of the day, 'How was he, today?' expecting the same extolling of virtues I'd had with the first. After a term of discussion about his unwillingness to follow the rules in the same way as his paragon of a brother I was pretty much at breaking point. I'd fret away all evening about how to solve this, until one night, it hit me that what I was actually trying to do was find a way to make him into a different person.

The next time I asked how he'd been and got the expected answer I said to the teacher, 'You know, I've finally reached the point where I no longer feel responsible for who he is as a person. I'm happy to work with you to find tools that will help him, but I don't feel I can change him.' To my surprise, his wonderful, and very experienced, teacher completely agreed with me. 'Well, of course,' she said. 'No one wants you to change who he is! He's a lovely boy, we just need to teach him to sit still and listen.' You see, sometimes the people who find it hardest to accept who our children are is us. Our emotional investment and apparent responsibility for their characters can blind us to the beauty of who they are as we busily work at managing how they are perceived.

On the flip side, every teacher has a war story about a parent who is so convinced that their child is perfect that they are wilfully blind to the problems their child is having or creating. Chrissie, a teacher for

14 years, finds this to be a growing part of classroom management. 'Over the last couple of years I've really noticed more and more parents refusing to accept that their children are wonderful, but flawed, mortals,' she says. ' I run into these parents who seem to think that their child is the only child in the class who matters and that every activity, problem or lesson must be run with their child's particular needs in mind and no one else's. It's as if they don't realise that there are at least 20 other kids in the class, all of whom are as real as their child. And if, God forbid, their child should be responsible for a problem at school all hell breaks loose. There's an automatic assumption that you, the teacher, or the other children have somehow caused the problem and that if only everyone else would change their behaviour to accommodate their child, there would be no problem. Maybe it's a knee-jerk thing to think, but I can't help noticing that as parents have got older and families smaller this attitude has become more and more pervasive.'

The enduring attitude that life is a race and the goal is to be a winner at all costs is a big part of the problem. One woman I spoke with recalled being taken aback by the intensity of the questions asked by parents at the kindergarten information night at her local primary school. 'I already knew I'd be sending Zac there,' says Heather. 'He was already at the preschool and it was the local school. I thought the night would be a chance for us to find out what we needed to do to enrol him and some tips for starting school. About ten minutes into the meeting it became really clear that for some of the parents this was a opportunity for the school to audition for the right to host their child. The poor principal hardly had a chance to give her presentation because the questions came like bullets. And they were so self-serving! Everybody had their own vested concern – sports or music or academic excellence – and just peppered her with questions. At first

I felt like a bit of a loser, like I wasn't taking Zac's schooling seriously enough. Then I started to feel shocked by the tone of these parents, and then angry. By the end of the night, the principal had even been attacked over the government's funding policies, as if she had anything to do with them! The next day I said to a friend I still liked the school but hated what these parents were saying and the way they'd set the tone. She just laughed and said, "Don't worry, you'll never see them again. They'll be too busy at work to spend any time at school and they'll leave all that boring daily stuff to you and me." It might sound snobby, but I hope she's right.'

Taking the conversation further, it became obvious that what had offended Heather was not so much the kind or amount of questions the parents had asked. 'I understand that people do things differently,' says Heather. 'When you're short of time and trying to make the best decision it makes sense to ask as many questions as possible. What got me was the attitude they were taking. It was like, "So sell it to me". I felt like saying, "This is a school, not a credit card." I think that some of them had forgotten that a local primary school is part of the community.'

A school is also a community in and of itself, and one that needs parents of all shapes and sizes. It's easy for the split between working and stay-at-home mums to flare up in the school arena. Resentment can be fostered when the same parents take responsibility for out-of-school activities, P&C duties, fetes, discos and classroom assistance. Those who are shouldering the practical burden can feel both abandoned and dismissed. Those who are constrained to fleeting visits by a busy work schedule can feel excluded from both the playground camaraderie and the decision-making. The truth is that schools need *all* their parents and each group provides a different kind of support, support that schools rely on.

'WHEN I WORKED FULL TIME I WOULD FLY PAST THE SCHOOL IN THE MORNINGS, HURL MY CHILDREN FROM THE CAR WITH A KISS AND A LUNCH ORDER AND THEN BATTLE THE MORNING TRAFFIC TO GET TO WORK ON TIME. AFTER A COUPLE OF YEARS OF THIS I WAS OFFERED THE OPPORTUNITY TO CHANGE CAREERS TO A JOB THAT OFFERED ME A LOT MORE FLEXIBILITY TO WORK FROM HOME. SUDDENLY, I FOUND MYSELF WITH TIME TO LINGER AT THE SCHOOL GATES, HELP IN THE CANTEEN AND JOIN THE P&C. ONE THING I WILL NEVER DO IS JOIN IN THE BITCHING AND WHINGEING ON EITHER SIDE OF THE FENCE; WORKING OR NOT, BUSY OR NOT, I WAS A GOOD MOTHER THEN, AND I'M STILL ONE NOW.'

The demands of the curriculum combined with the financial constraints of the funding formula leave many schools dependent on the financial and practical goodwill of their parent body. In my admittedly short parental career I've been both a rarely glimpsed full-time toiler and the full-time mama who makes up the numbers so the kids can go to the library. Right now, I'm a little bit of both, and I just left the computer for a couple of hours to help a neighbour slice and dice vast quantities of vegetables for Monday's canteen meal deal.

Elaine works ostensibly four days a week but effectively five. 'The business is mine and my husband's,' she says, 'and I guess I've been lucky. It meant I could take some time off when the girls were really little. Now the business needs me, but so do the girls, so I do what I can when I can.'

When it comes to parental support and assistance at schools, that's what it should come down to: each of us giving as much or as little as we can, or feel comfortable with, and all of us respecting the choices and needs of our fellow parents. Make your choices and stand by them, have faith in yourself and confidence in your ability to make the right decisions for you and your children and, with a little bit of luck, you should all make it through school relatively unscathed.

'Education is for improving the life of others and for leaving your community and world better than you found it.'
MARIAN WRIGHT EDELMAN

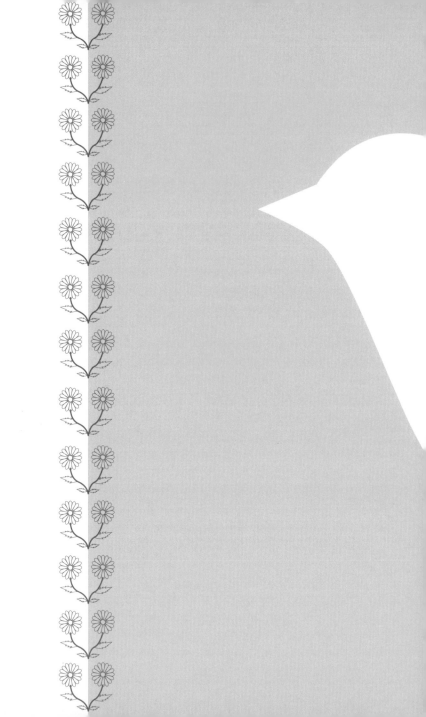

Backwards and in high heels

'A HOUSE DOESN'T NEED A
WIFE ANY MORE THAN IT
NEEDS A HUSBAND.'

CHARLOTTE PERKINS GILMAN

Household affairs

'One of the advantages of being disorderly is that one is constantly making exciting discoveries.'

A.A. MILNE

Sharing the load is a wonderful concept, isn't it? Happy couples twirling through the intricate steps of running a house like a couple of ballroom dancers gliding through a waltz. Unfortunately, statistics reveal that, like many of the best concepts, this one never made it off the drawing board. And how scary are those statistics? Well, in Australia at any rate, whether or not a woman works outside the home, she shoulders around 70 per cent of the housework and childcare. Call me naïve, but I had no inkling that one little baby would lead to a tripling in the domestic chore load, nor did I expect to shoulder so much of it on my own. And being a seriously slow learner, it simply never occurred to me that each extra child has an exponential effect on the housework bell curve. Sometimes I look around the house and feel like I'm keeping house for an army of malicious gremlins. Then I realise that I'm actually keeping house and the horror of it sends me to the couch, glass in hand, wondering what happened to my modern, emancipated life.

I always assumed that my beloved and I would share the burden of daily life in an equitable, unspoken way, that we'd smile at each other as I washed and he dried, chat while we folded the children's collection of clothing and tacitly take on board those tasks that the other simply couldn't face (taking out the rubbish on my part and changing sheets on his). Actually, I lie, as I never ever even once looked into the future and thought about the housework. But as the domestic burden of family life slipped inevitably over us, these were the assumptions that fed my vision of how things would be, should be but, of course, never were.

'BELIEVE IT OR NOT, I DON'T REALLY LIKE HOUSEWORK, BUT I CAN'T STAND LIVING IN CHAOS. THINGS ARE BUSY AROUND HERE AND UNLESS THE HOUSE IS BASICALLY ORDERED, IT'S IMPOSSIBLE TO GET ANYTHING DONE. I ACCEPT THAT KIDS ARE MESSY CREATURES BUT I'M DOING MY BEST TO TRAIN THEM AS I CAN'T AFFORD STAFF. WHAT I CAN'T ACCEPT IS THAT MY HUSBAND SEEMS TO THINK HE IS EXCUSED WHEN IT COMES TO HOUSEWORK. OKAY, SO HE'S AT WORK ALL DAY, SO I COP THE BULK OF THE WORK IN DAYLIGHT HOURS, BUT WHAT'S HIS EXCUSE WHEN THE SUN GOES DOWN?

'THE BIG DEAL FOR ME HAS NOTHING TO DO WITH HIM TIDYING UP, NO, IT'S ABOUT HIM MESSING UP. I CAN'T BELIEVE HOW MUCH WORK HE CREATES IN AN AVERAGE EVENING, AND IT JUST DOESN'T OCCUR TO HIM TO CLEAN IT UP. WE USED TO FIGHT ABOUT IT CONSTANTLY UNTIL

ONE DAY I SAID, "YOU KNOW WHAT? YOU CARRY ON AS YOU ARE, BUT GIVE ME THE KEY TO YOUR OFFICE." HE WAS LIKE, "WHAT THE HELL ARE YOU ON ABOUT?". I JUST EXPLAINED THAT WHILE HE WAS BUSY TRASHING THE HOUSE, I'D POP INTO THE OFFICE, HURL ALL HIS PAPERS IN THE AIR AND TOMORROW MORNING WE COULD START THE DAY ON A LEVEL PLAYING FIELD. I COULD ACTUALLY SEE THE PENNY DROP AND SINCE THEN HE'S BEEN, WELL, NOT PERFECT, BUT TOLERABLE.'

When I plotted out the chapters for this book I knew that at some stage I'd have to tackle the issue of housework. I also knew I'd probably leave it for as long as possible. To me it's a bit like the second drawer in the kitchen – such a tangled mess, I'm rarely brave enough to do more than dart in, grab what I need and slam it shut, swearing to myself I'll get it sorted just as soon as I have the time. I also swore to myself that I wouldn't allow this chapter to descend into some kind of general whinge about men, in particular the men we share our houses and, ostensibly our housework, with. Problem was, it was hard to find anybody who felt that they had managed to find an equitable way to split the load with their partner.

There seems to be a general feeling, and it's one that I find hard to argue with, that when it comes to the business of the home, most men just aren't pulling their weight. Worse than that, no one seems to have a solution to what is one of the most common areas of conflict in domestic relationships. Several years ago a British minister suggested that many marriages could be saved if only people were prepared to fork out 50 quid on a weekly cleaner. Among the predictable howls of outrage, no one seemed to give voice to my main objection, not just the matter of who cleans for the cleaner, but how anyone can reduce the task of managing a household to a few bits of obvious cleaning.

'IT'S NOT JUST HOUSEWORK THAT CAUSES PROBLEMS IN OUR
RELATIONSHIP, IT'S THE ISSUE OF WHO TAKES RESPONSIBILITY FOR
WHAT, ESPECIALLY ON WEEKDAY MORNINGS. PROBLEM IS, CARL
SEEMS TO THINK THAT HE IS ONLY RESPONSIBLE FOR HIMSELF, AND
THE REST OF IT IS UP TO ME. WHEN HE HAS EARLY MEETINGS I'M
COOL WITH IT, BUT THE REST OF THE TIME? I'LL BE DOING THE
NORMAL ROUTINE OF LOOKING AFTER EVERYONE WHILE HE GETS UP,
HAS BREAKFAST, GOES BACK TO BED WITH IT TO WATCH THE BUSINESS
NEWS, HAS A SHOWER AND SWINGS OUT THE DOOR. I'VE TRIED
GETTING HIM TO CHANGE BUT IT JUST LEADS TO MASSIVE FIGHTS, SO
NOW I JUST COP IT IN THE NAME OF A PEACEFUL MORNING. IT'S THAT
OR START FANTASISING ABOUT DIVORCE.'

If keeping house were as simple as cleaning the toilet, it wouldn't be
the burning issue it so patently is. Besides the endless to-do list,
which we'll get to later, there is the matter of responsibility. Men who
abdicate responsibility for the tasks involved in running a household
are turning their partners into their mothers. Behaving as though the
bin only needs emptying because you want it done, not because it is
full, is just one of the fun ways some men shift full accountability onto
the shoulders of their partners. These are no longer the days of men
working nine to five while the little woman dons an apron and
communes with her appliances, except when it comes to cleaning the
fridge. I have a postcard on my long-suffering fridge with an
illustration of a classic 1950s housewife inhabiting her kitchen with
pride and just a little bit of resignation. Across the bottom it says, 'The
thought of another Sunday lunch made her crave a Prozac soufflé'.

The great housework conundrum epitomises the difference between
having it all and doing it all. Choosing to work outside the home offers
no protection against the hungry washing machine waiting at home.

Statistics show that when both partners work, the average man does seven hours of housework per week to the woman's 18 hours. There's something really wrong with that picture, and it's going to take more powerful tools than a nag and a whinge to do something about it.

'IT'S NOT THAT PAUL DOESN'T DO MUCH AROUND THE HOUSE, IT'S MORE THAT HE DOESN'T DO ANYTHING. PRE-KIDS I JUST NEVER NOTICED BECAUSE, FRANKLY, THE TWO OF US DIDN'T MAKE A LOT OF MESS. I'D GO TO WORK CLOSING THE DOOR ON A PRETTY, ORDERED HOUSE AND OPEN THE DOOR TO THE SAME SCENE THAT EVENING, BUT WITH THREE KIDS, LOOKING AFTER THE HOUSE HAS BECOME A FULL-TIME JOB THAT I SEEM TO HAVE TO FIT IN ON TOP OF MY ACTUAL FULL-TIME JOB. AT FIRST I JUST DID IT ALL, THINKING HE'D SEE WHAT A STRUGGLE IT WAS AND START TO HELP OUT. FORGET ABOUT IT; I EVEN REALISED THAT HE CAME HOME LATE EVERY TUESDAY RATHER THAN BE THERE ON TIME TO TAKE THE RUBBISH OUT. THEN I STARTED TO ASK HIM TO DO MORE, WHICH QUICKLY TURNED INTO NAGGING. HE FELT NAGGED AND I FELT LIKE A NAG AND HATED IT.

'SO I STARTED DOING IT ALL AGAIN BUT JUST FELT SICK WITH RESENTMENT SO MUCH OF THE TIME THAT IT STARTED TO REALLY AFFECT OUR MARRIAGE. THEN, ONE NIGHT, STRAIGHT AFTER SEX, I PROPOSED A DAY SWAP. I SAID, "ALRIGHT, PAUL, TOMORROW, JUST FOR ONE DAY, I'M GOING TO BE YOU AND YOU BE ME FROM BREAKFAST TO BEDTIME". I COULDN'T BELIEVE IT WHEN HE AGREED, MUST HAVE BEEN THE AFTERGLOW! SO THE NEXT MORNING THE ALARM WENT AT 6.30 AND I KICKED HIM AWAKE AND POINTED OUT IT WAS TIME TO TAKE DAFFY THE DOG OUT FOR HER MORNING WEE. HE TRIED TO CALL ON NINA TO DO IT BUT I INSISTED THAT HE HAD TO DO IT MY WAY AND I'D DO HIS SHARE HIS WAY. SO HE GOT UP TO DO IT, MUTTERING AWAY, AND THEN CAME BACK TO THE BEDROOM WITH THE PAPER AND STARTED TO

GET INTO BED. I SNATCHED THE PAPER AND ASKED WHEN MY COFFEE WOULD BE READY. THEN I SPENT ABOUT 40 MINUTES IN BED READING THE PAPER AND DRINKING COFFEE, HAD A SHOWER, BREAKFAST AND A CIGARETTE ON THE TERRACE IN MY DRESSING GOWN WHILE HE DRESSED THE GIRLS, MADE BREAKFAST AND LUNCHES, PACKED BAGS AND SWORE UNDER HIS BREATH. WHEN I FINALLY SAUNTERED DOWN AT TEN TO NINE, DRESSED AND REFRESHED, TO RUN THE GIRLS TO SCHOOL, HE ASKED ME TO DROP HIM AT WORK ON THE WAY. I THOUGHT HE WAS GOING TO KILL ME WHEN I POINTED OUT THAT HE NEEDED TO TIDY UP THE MORNING CHAOS BEFORE HE LEFT SO HE SHOULD PROBABLY JUST WALK AND MEET ME AT THE OFFICE. THEN I SWANNED OFF WITH THE GIRLS, DROPPED THEM AT SCHOOL AND PICKED UP A COFFEE ON MY WAY TO WORK. I FELT LIKE A BIT OF A BITCH BUT I ALSO FELT FANTASTIC. I STARTED THE DAY IN BETTER SHAPE THAN I COULD REMEMBER AND DEFINITELY GOT THE MESSAGE THROUGH AT THE SAME TIME.'

It's easy to bitch and joke about men and housework, and believe me, we will, but making light of it ignores the negative impact it can have on family happiness and a woman's career. Trying to run a house devoid of order is like going into battle without a plan; I know, because I've done it. It took me a long time to get the hang of keeping the house even vaguely tidy, let alone operational. If anyone dropped by for a surprise visit they could count on being greeted by a kitchen full of dirty dishes, strategic mountains of clean and dirty clothing and a cunning obstacle course of toys and books. The turning point came about 18 months ago. An imposed period of coping on my own meant that I either got a grip and learnt to be tidy or we were all going down. It's amazing what you can do when you put your mind to it. My shoddy housekeeping was so infamous that friends are still surprised by the order and calm, but I can no longer live without it.

Problem is that getting into housework is a bit like getting into drugs – you know one leads to another and before you know it, you're hooked on the hard stuff. Once I got my house really clean for the first time, I discovered there was this whole other layer of undisturbed dirt and disorder lying just under the surface, waiting to trap the unwary. Before you know it, it's not enough for the kitchen counters to be clean; you need to know that behind the doors unseen order reigns. Cleaning the fridge from top to bottom leads you to discover that under your fridge is a whole new ecosystem of dirt that may be unseen but must be conquered. That way lies the 'second drawer' and madness, and the expectation that others will live up to your newfound standards. Which leads to conflict and to, oh, you having to take some responsibility for the great housework rift. Damn.

'I HEAR GIRLFRIENDS WHINGEING ABOUT MESSY HUSBANDS AND I JUST THINK, "GOD, I SHOULD BE SO LUCKY!" DAVID, MY HUSBAND, IS MR ANAL WHEN IT COMES TO HOUSEWORK WHILE I AM COMPLETELY DOMESTICALLY BLIND. IT WOULDN'T MATTER IF HE WOULD JUST ACCEPT MY EFFORTS, BUT WHEN I TRY TO CLEAN SOMETHING IT'S NEVER GOOD ENOUGH AND I GET ANOTHER LITTLE LESSON ON HOW TO DO IT RIGHT. HE'S GOT BETTER OVER THE YEARS, BUT WE STILL CAN'T DO ANYTHING AS A FAMILY ON A SATURDAY MORNING UNTIL THE WHOLE HOUSE IS SANITISED AND GLEAMING.'

'My husband and I have never considered divorce ... murder sometimes, but never divorce.'

JOYCE BROTHERS

Standards differ from house to house, person to person; one person's squalor is another's creative clutter. Despite my newfound status as a paragon of cleanliness I have a friend who can't bring herself to take a seat in my house without surreptitiously dusting it off. I, on the other hand, find her house so clean it's scary – once I've finished my drink I can't work up the nerve to put the glass down in case I mark the surfaces. She could never live with my standards, nor I with hers, but we respect each other's right to be crazy by our own standards. In an ideal world, the same respect would extend into marriages and partnerships. You like it spick and span, he couldn't care less, so you agree on a minimum standard and anything above and beyond that is fair game. Unfortunately, negotiating that one can make the Geneva Convention look like a document composed by lightweights. So what to do if all else fails? Call in the kids, they're the ones who make most of the mess in the first place. You might as well exploit them while you've got them and lighten the load all round.

KIDS' CHORES

Kids doing chores around the house was once a given. Responsibility was learned, pocket money was earned and children were equipped for the great adventure of future independence. It's amazing how many children are excused, in fact excluded, from the running of the house these days. It's easy to go down the 'in my day' route, but doing chores was fun. In my day, we had a roster for small jobs like setting the table and washing the dishes, plus one large age-appropriate job that was our permanent responsibility. Mine was the ironing – all of our ironing – Mum, Dad and four kids, all of whom were kitted out in full private-school regalia. I've still not forgiven my mother for that, and I refuse to iron to this day, but I doubt she feels sorry for me. In her day she would have shouldered a much bigger load, and her mother even more. Children lucky enough to be spared the mines were still expected to wash the dishes at four years of age; my six-year-old still calls out imperiously whenever he wants something, like I'm the butler.

'THREE BOYS MAKE A LOT OF MESS, AND WITH THE HOURS MY HUSBAND WORKS IT'S UP TO ME TO DEAL WITH MOST OF IT, DESPITE THE FACT I WORK. ONE NIGHT IT JUST FELT LIKE THE LOAD WAS TOO HEAVY, IT WAS RAINING AND THE BOYS HAD TRACKED MUD EVERYWHERE, THEY'D THROWN THEIR PYJAMAS ON THE FLOOR INSTEAD OF PUTTING THEM ON AND, TO TOP IT OFF, THEY'D UNMADE MY BED. ALL I WANTED TO DO WAS GET EVERYTHING FINISHED SO I COULD SIT DOWN FOR A WHILE. SO I LOST IT; I YELLED AT THEM, TOLD THEM THAT THEY HAD TO HELP ME, NOT MAKE IT HARDER, AND THEN WENT TO THE BATHROOM TO HAVE A LITTLE CRY.

'SUDDENLY, I HEARD THE VACUUM GOING AND WHEN I CAME OUT TO INVESTIGATE I FOUND ALL THREE PROPERLY DRESSED AND THE OLDEST VACUUMING THE LIVING ROOM WHILE THE TWO LITTLE ONES CAREFULLY AND CLUMSILY REMADE MY BED. THEY LOOKED SO SHEEPISH AND ANGELIC I JUST THOUGHT "BUGGER THE HOUSE" AND WE ALL CLIMBED INTO MY BED TO CUDDLE AND READ.'

Pocket money and jobs have finally been instituted at the behest of the eldest, not because he wanted the responsibility, but he was pretty keen on the reward and offered up the deal in a fine show of early negotiation skills. He seemed to think that $10 per job was pretty fair, he was also happy to pick the jobs as he went along. We bartered him down to $2 a week for setting the table, clearing the dishes and picking up after himself – clothes in the basket, shoes on the verandah, towel on the rail. There was a mild panic when we discovered that $2 would essentially limit him to lollies, as a basic children's mag starts at $4.50. So we upped his pocket money to $5 a week and now everybody's happy. But it got me thinking, why did it take us so long to start expecting the children to help us with household chores?

In some ways we are raising one of the most coddled generations in history – not only are they chauffeured, entertained and stimulated, they are rarely required to pick up after themselves until well into adolescence (by which time it's probably too late anyway). Then I thought, 'Maybe I'm being a little harsh; I'm tired, it's late, I have to finish this chapter, do some washing and stack the dishwasher before I go to bed.' Next, I wondered why I was still working and doing housework on the scary side of midnight, which led to me examining our day. Just an average day, school, and work, then yoga for the littlest and art class for the other two while I shop for dinner. Then home, dinner, homework, bath, reading, a quick play, then stories and sleep. There was no time for housework, or work work, for either them or me. Our time was accounted for right up until they slipped into the land of nod.

So where has all the time gone? We did activities after school, sport, pottery classes, German, whatever was going, really, and we had homework, but we somehow had more time, which Mum was happy to fill with the odd chore if we were silly enough to get in the way. Our kids' time has gone the same way as ours; it's been eaten up by the commute, defeated by the tyranny of the car. Not every day is the same; there are still days when we wander home from school together and just kind of schlep around and I fully intend to fill them with a variety of delightful chores. But the days we get into the car after school are the days we say goodbye to leisurely activity and hello whirlwind.

So I searched my conscience and my schedule to come up with a way to build some kind of helpful activity into even the busiest day without pushing anyone, and especially not me, over the edge. When I couldn't find a solution I did what I always do and browsed the fridge and there was the answer staring me in the face – dinner. We always eat it, I usually cook it and they always hang around moaning that they're hungry – it was the perfect opportunity. I'll be honest and admit that cooking with my kids is not quite like a scene from Nigella Lawson or Bill Granger, or even Jamie Oliver. Little fingers and sharp knives are a scary combination, but the kids are so excited about being involved they just ache to ape whatever I'm doing. One or the other might wander off midway through and then return, but, by the time the meal is cooked, they've all helped out in one way or another. The best thing is, they're prepared to eat just about anything they've helped to cook and that combined with their natural inclination to experiment has widened our weekly menu considerably. There have been a few disasters, but what's life without the odd disaster?

'MY GRANDPARENTS HAD A CATTLE FARM AND I'D SPEND EVERY HOLIDAY ROAMING AROUND, HELPING OUT AND EXPLORING. GRANNY KEPT A PROPER VEGETABLE GARDEN AND I USED TO LOVE HELPING HER PICK AND POD THE PEAS. WE'D SIT IN THE SUNROOM WITH A BOWL BETWEEN US AND EAT AS WE WENT. WHENEVER I WANT TO CAPTURE THAT FEELING OF TIME AND TRADITION WITH INGRID AND ROBYN, I BUY A BIG BAG OF PEAS FROM THE GROCERS AND WE SIT AND POD THEM TOGETHER.'

'In my day, we didn't have self-esteem, we had self-respect, and no more of it than we had earned.'

JANE HADDAM

Housework doesn't have to be a battleground with kids. The younger they are, the more willing and easily trained they are, so get them started early. It also doesn't have to be practical – one rainy day I took down the silver, gave each of them a cloth and promised prizes to the one who did the most. Of course, in my eyes they'd all done as well as each other, so everyone got a prize and I got some almost-polished silver. One friend got her son to put their chaotic CD collection in alphabetical order. He got all the way to F before he gave up and then came back, suitably bribed, to finish it the following day. There are many ways to involve your kids in running the house with a minimum of trauma and maximum results for all. We owe it to ourselves, our children and their subsequent partners to make sure that our offspring are housetrained. If current trends are any indication, they'll probably still be living with us when they're 40, but at least they'll be useful around the house.

> '*Becoming responsible adults is no longer a matter of whether children hang up their pyjamas or put dirty towels in the hamper, but whether they care about themselves and others and whether they see everyday chores as related to how we treat this planet.*'
>
> EDIE LESHAN

There was an email joke doing the rounds last year. It was real enough to be funny and went something like this:

> 'A MAN COMES HOME FROM WORK ONE DAY TO FIND HIS CHILDREN HALF-NAKED AND DIRTY, RUNNING AROUND THE GARDEN THROWING MUD AT EACH OTHER. THE FRONT DOOR IS WIDE OPEN AND INSIDE HE IS GREETED BY A SCENE OF TOTAL CHAOS. THE FURNITURE IS PUSHED AROUND AND SOME OF IT IS LYING ON THE GROUND. THERE IS FOOD EVERYWHERE, ON THE SOFA, THE WALLS, EVEN THE CEILING. EVERYWHERE HE LOOKS THERE IS TURMOIL AND DISORDER, MOST WORRYING OF ALL, HIS WIFE IS NOWHERE TO BE FOUND. HE GOES RUNNING THROUGH THE HOUSE, CALLING HER NAME, AND FINDS HER CURLED UP IN BED WITH A CUP OF COFFEE AND A GOOD BOOK. HE CRIES OUT, "MY GOD, JANE, WHAT HAPPENED: ARE YOU ALRIGHT?" SHE LOOKS UP, SMILES AND SAYS, "YOU KNOW HOW YOU COME HOME AND ASK WHAT I DID ALL DAY? WELL TODAY, I DIDN'T DO IT."'

If you really wanted to stretch it to cover all the nameless things that are done in the average day, you'd need to stretch this quiet rebellion over a much longer time frame. Picture the wife saying, 'To hell with the to-do list, I'm just going to go with the flow'. Three months later, when she finally takes to her bed in protest at the fact that no one's even noticed, the kids aren't just filthy, they're also nurturing a splendid crop of dental caries. The house isn't just a mess, it's cold and dark because the power and the phone have been cut off due to unpaid bills. It's also damp, thanks to overflowing gutters and a leak left unrepaired. The fridge has stopped working because no one has defrosted the freezer and, to top it all off, the dog's gone missing as the gate was left open. Don't misread this as a claim that only women take care of these tasks. It's more a reminder, which you probably don't need, that there's more to running the house than the cleaning, and to forget that that leads to more unfairness and greater resentment. Unless someone does all the nameless boring stuff, the ship will spring a leak and sink under the weight of neglect.

How do you share it out without tears and tantrums? I don't know, but I do know one couple who have got closer than anyone I know. Instead of allocating tasks, they claim them. Once a month they sit down and compile a list of all waiting tasks, big and small. Then, like picking a team, they take it in turns to choose a task from the list until they reach the end. The deal is that by the next month's meeting each of them will have checked and ticked their list and, in the meantime, neither is allowed to check on the other's progress. It works for them, they both take responsibility and leave resentment behind. Would it work for us? I don't know, I'm still trying to get my hubby to give it a go.

'REMEMBER, GINGER ROGERS DID
EVERYTHING FRED ASTAIRE DID,
BUT SHE DID IT BACKWARDS AND
IN HIGH HEELS.'

FAITH WHITTLESEY

Working for a living

'I've yet to hear a man ask for advice on how to combine marriage and a career.'

GLORIA STEINEM

Okay, can we stop now with the working-mothers-versus-non-working-mothers thing? I forget that the debate continues to exist at all and get a shock whenever it rears its ugly head. So, let's just get a few things out of the way straight up. Number one, there is no such thing as a non-working mother, only mothers who work exclusively in the home and those who work both inside and out. Number two, we are not just mothers for the first few years of our children's lives, we will be mothers for as long as we still have children, right up until the day we die and, really, how many of us will spend 50 years at home? Number three, your choice works for you (or at least it should) and your neighbour's choice works for her; neither of you is a better mother and you are both doing it your own way. Now I've got that out of my system we can move on to the really tricky stuff. Unfortunately, that means just about everything when it comes to the issues of motherhood and work. It's a classic damned-if-you-do, damned-if-you-don't situation.

Politicians have a phrase for an issue considered to be a no-brainer. They call it a 'motherhood' issue, the assumption being that there is one, obvious, response that will satisfy everybody and ignite no controversy. Ironically, the opposite is true when it comes to discussion of modern-day working motherhood. It seems that everybody has such strong opinions on whether, when and how mothers should work that it can be hard to hear you own voice through the din.

The days of mama trussed up in a floral-patterned housecoat behind her white picket fence are long gone. Now there are as many ways of being a mother as there are mothers, and no matter what choices a woman makes as she goes about her daily business, you can be sure that someone, somewhere feels free to criticise. Mothers today are the inheritors of the 'you can be anything' message, the successors of those trailblazers who liberated women from their kitchens. Or so we're told; for most women, the choices they make in order to balance their lives are simply that – their choices.

To work or not to work is merely the beginning of the journey and is, of itself, a condescending question that denies mothering the status of work. Childcare, nannies, quality time, domestic chores, your partner's work, family maintenance and still finding time for a real relationship are just some of the pieces in the motherhood puzzle. If it's hard putting them together in the first place, throwing a paid job into the mix can turn a precariously balanced life into chaos. But it can also turn a creaking edifice into a well-oiled machine. You see, somewhere, in the midst of all that juggling and caring, there's also the small matter of your personal happiness. Making it work for your family must, at some stage, also involve making it work for you. All you have to do is find the unique and naturally symbiotic system that allows you and your tribe to flourish and thrive and all will be well. Simple, really, so how come it can be so bloody hard and scary and pressured?

It would be blind and arrogant to assume that working after childbirth is always a matter of choice, but it seems there are plenty of visually impaired types out there. There are those who take issue with the idea that any mother needs to work. Somehow managing to discount the entire population of single mothers, they claim that the financial pressure we endure is self-inflicted and that if we were only sensible and self-sacrificing enough to choose to live a different life, we could all happily live on our (presumed) partner's income. Apparently, there's an undiscovered stock of easily affordable family homes and if we could just give up our plasma-screen habit, we'd be laughing.

SEARCHING FOR SUPERWOMAN

'Working mother' has somehow become synonymous with 'super-woman'. There's a pervasive fantasy that post-partum women are tossing up between running a gracious home and returning to an unutterably fabulous job. The reality for most of us is less a glossy magazine spread and more a hastily read sheet of newspaper. That sheet of paper may be spotted with crumbs and the smears of tiny fingers, but it's our piece of paper and it can morph from a jaunty paper hat to a handy mop. In other less confusing, words, the life we have is the one we have to work with, but what we make of it is partly up to us and partly a result of necessity.

'IT DIDN'T OCCUR TO ME TO STOP WORKING. I THINK THAT PERSONALLY I'M A BETTER MOTHER AND SPOUSE BECAUSE I DO WORK. I'M NOT PROUD OF THE FACT I'M NOT SATISFIED BEING JUST AT HOME, BUT I ACCEPT IT. I'M NOT GOOD AT DOING THAT PUZZLE FOR THE EIGHTEENTH TIME, BUT WHEN I'M HOME I DRINK AVA IN AND GIVE HER TOTAL ACCESS TO ME. THERE ARE NO PHONES, NO INTRUSIONS. I THINK IF I WERE AT HOME ALL THE TIME I'D BE SMOTHERING HER; IT WOULD BECOME ABOUT ME TRYING TO MAKE HER PERFECT. I HAVE TO BE STRETCHED, KIND OF SPREAD THIN, OR IT'S NOT PRETTY.'

Knowing yourself and your options are the key ingredients in making decisions about employment and I find hope and flexibility excellent seasonings to keep on hand for emergency situations. Maternity leave is the first obstacle most women have to tackle when it comes to mixing with both babies and the boss. The fact that, in this country at least, it's unpaid makes it a crunchy one for many of us and can act as a deterrent to going back for some women.

'Once we'd adjusted to the drop in income there just didn't seem to be much point in going back to work,' says Miriam. 'I'd never really settled into a career and didn't particularly like my job. For me, working was about making the money to buy clothes and go out. Those things weren't on the table after I'd had Willem anyway, so I just let the job go and settled into being at home with him.' Others find the complete opposite, that the drain on the family finances is so acute that going back to work sooner rather than later is the only option.

'I've always pulled in a higher salary than Dominic,' says Maria. 'I'm a lawyer and he's a social worker, so staying at home was never an option for me. I'm lucky enough to work for a fairly enlightened employer who agreed to pay a portion of my wage for six months, or we would have been well and truly stuffed.'

Not all companies provide a workable or welcoming environment for mothers returning to the workforce and there are some entire industries that, by virtue of the hours or tasks required, would seem to exclude women with children altogether. Yet take a closer look and you'll find working mothers just about everywhere, from the houses of parliament to the beat of a cop on the street. There's an enormous amount of ingenuity, creativity and plain hard work being expended by mothers everywhere and every day. Just to get to work requires a battle plan that can make tackling the job itself seem like a breeze in comparison, at least until you run into your first problem of the day.

There's also an enormous amount of anger out there, tainting the positive benefits of work for a lot of employed mothers. It's enough to be juggling the load of family and work without having to tackle the perception that we are somehow a burden in the workplace. It has become acceptable to treat working mothers as though they are a troublesome and demanding minority rather than just another facet of the workforce. While compiling the research for this book I received a passionate and articulate email that summed up the bitter heart of the workplace environment confronting many of us better than I ever could. So here it is:

'I HAVE LONG THOUGHT THAT THE SUPERMOM SCARY SHOULDER-PADDED CAREER WOMAN WHO HAPPENED TO HAVE CHILDREN AT HOME IN A CUPBOARD SOMEWHERE DURING THE 80S HAS NOW GIVEN WAY TO A NEW GENERATION OF OVER-ACHIEVING WOULD-BE EARTH MOTHERS WHO ARE TRYING TO DO IT ALL. AND DOING QUITE A REASONABLE JOB OF IT TOO, ACTUALLY.

'IT'S ALL V. WELL THAT WE'VE BECOME ORGANICALLY AWARE. IT'S ALL V. WELL THAT WE ARE NOW MORE INVOLVED WITH OUR CHILDREN'S EDUCATIONAL DEVELOPMENT, AND MORE INFORMED ON ISSUES RELATING TO THEIR EMOTIONAL AND PERSONAL DEVELOPMENT. AND IT'S ALL V. WELL THAT WE ARE "ENCOURAGED" (WHERE NOT JUST FISCALLY OBLIGED) TO MAINTAIN SOME INVOLVEMENT IN THE WORKFORCE IN PARALLEL WITH OUR MOTHERING ROLE. IT'S EVEN ALL V. WELL THAT THE EMPLOYMENT MARKET IS SO MUCH MORE AWARE OF THE GREAT RESOURCE THAT RESTS IN THE MOTHERING COMMUNITY AND IS KEENER ON PART-TIME AND EVEN WORK-FROM-HOME ARRANGEMENTS.

'OF COURSE THEY'RE KEENER. THEY GET HIGHLY EXPERIENCED AND QUALIFIED SKIVVIES WHO WORK LIKE DOGS, ARE STATISTICALLY PROVEN TO BE UNDERPAID RELATIVE TO THEIR MALE COUNTERPARTS, AND CONSTANTLY FEEL GUILTY AND OVER-APPRECIATIVE. THESE WOMEN NEVER FEEL THEY'RE DOING ANY JOB IN ANY PART OF THEIR LIVES WELL. THEY ARE EASY TO MANAGE BECAUSE THEY LACK THE CONFIDENCE IN THEIR SITUATIONS TO AGITATE FOR BETTER EMPLOYMENT CONDITIONS, AND THEY ACTIVELY AVOID PROMOTION BECAUSE THE KNIFE-EDGE UPON WHICH THEIR LIVES ARE SO FINELY BALANCED SIMPLY WOULD NOT ACCOMMODATE FURTHER RESPONSIBILITY.

'MANY ACTUALLY ACCEPT LESSER JOBS AT LESSER PAY WHEN THEY RETURN. THEY NEVER TAKE LUNCH BREAKS. THEY NEVER STAND BY THE WATER COOLER GOSSIPING. THEY INSTEAD SQUEEZE FIVE DAYS WORK INTO THREE, AND THEN SPEND THE OTHER TWO "QUALITY-TIME" DAYS, DOING ALL THE HOUSEHOLD CHORES, CHILD IN TOW, WITH THE OFFICE HAUNTING THEM VIA MOBILE AND EMAIL ALL THE WHILE. WHENEVER THE PHONE RINGS AT WORK, AND IT'S THE SCHOOL, THEY GO INTO PAROXYSMS OF STRESS OVER HOW THEY'RE GOING TO MANAGE WORK COMMITMENTS AND A SICK KID. IF THEY'RE REQUIRED TO

ATTEND A MEETING ON THEIR "DAY OFF", THEN THERE ARE
PAROXYSMS OF STRESS OVER HOW TO MANAGE THAT. MEANWHILE, HAS
FATHERING CHANGED ENOUGH TO COMPENSATE? THOUGH THERE'S
PROGRESS, I'M NOT SURE IT HAS OR CAN. AS I WRITE, I HAVE A
PARTICULAR DEAR FRIEND IN MIND, BUT I AM SURE BETWEEN US WE
COULD EACH NAME A DOZEN, REALLY.'

For me, the outrage lies not just in the conditions described above,
but in the attitude towards the women who live like this. Rather than
appreciation for managing such a load and doing a fabulous job
anyway, there is too often a pervasive whiff of disdain for the
mechanics of mothering floating around the office. 'My industry is
generally full of young people,' says Kelly, 'so as a mother, I'm a bit of
a novelty. I get the whole "I-don't-know-how-you-do-it!" thing all the
time, and work is generally pretty supportive. But I still have to
disguise my "mothering". You know, it's somehow okay to book a hair
appointment during office hours and then stay a bit late, so if I'm
taking Timmy to the dentist, I'll say I'm having a facial, and no one
blinks an eye.'

What's striking about this, and is beautifully encapsulated in the email
above, is the extent to which mothers are prepared to collude in the
downgrading of their status in the workplace. It starts before
breeding, and rapidly worsens in its wake. If you have any doubt that
gender inequality is still alive in the workplace, take a look at one very
telling indicator – comparative rates of pay. 'Equal pay for an equal
day's work' was a rallying call for our feminist forebears, yet many of
us seem content to take what we are offered and leave it at that. Even
more disturbing than apathy is the lack of self-belief it reflects.
Feeling as though you are lucky just to have your job is not exactly a
solid base from which to fight for more.

Remember how hard you worked to get where you are, add on how much more you are doing to maintain the pace and remind yourself you deserve respect and fair remuneration. You're not lucky to have the job, they are lucky to have you, your skills and your stamina.

No one is going to change the attitude towards working mothers, except for those women themselves. There's nothing in it for anyone else, it's a competitive world out there, and if they can knock you off the rung simply for who you are, they will. So hang in there and feel free to demand the recognition you deserve. It's the message we're giving our daughters, and our sons, so practise what you preach.

Confidence and the balls to tackle the boys at their own game seem to be the strategies employed by the working mothers who reported the greatest satisfaction with their situation. 'I was the first female partner in my firm to have a baby,' says Eliza. 'There were no precedents and no policy, so my managing partner and I had to work it out between us. He was very open in his approach and obviously concerned with getting me back to work and making sure I was happy to be there. I have always over-delivered at work so I knew I was in a position to ask for what I felt I needed. I just approached the negotiation in the same way I would any other aspect of my employment contract.'

Knowing that you are a valuable asset to the company is one thing, having the self-confidence to exploit it another. Prue, a senior associate in a large law firm, decided to plan and structure her post-partum future at work as strategically as she would any other project. 'I felt that by treating my negotiations over maternity leave and my subsequent position in an objective manner I would be able to achieve a better outcome.'

Others go even further by refusing to engage in the debate at all. 'My job is intense but, as a single mother, there was never any question as to whether or not I'd go back,' says Annabelle. 'Television is a consuming industry, but I'd always been really firm about managing my own time. I've always let the quality of my work speak for itself, and I felt no need to change that after Elias was born.'

It's not an easy trick to pull off and few of us have the courage to do it. The enormous benefit for Annabelle was that she wasted no energy on issues she considered to be extraneous. 'You know, I think the whole thing is a bit of a furphy, just another trick designed to keep women down,' she says. 'People have always had non-work commitments and they always will. There have always been workplaces that accommodate them and those where you have to fight for the right, but few people have been sacked for going to the dentist. Why should the fact that I'm meeting my child's needs be any different? I care intensely about my work and I've never been prepared to do anything but the best possible job. Why should that be any different now that I'm a mother? The thing is, I'm just not prepared to waste my energy having the fight, so I just behave as though it's already won.'

Not every workplace and not every job is going to be equally accommodating. There comes a time for some of us when the work environment becomes so discouraging that the options are to fight the company through the courts, or choose to move on. There are others for whom there are no real options at all. This country, like most, is serviced and maintained by a vast army of low-paid, casual workers, many of whom are mothers. The answer to the problems of mass exploitation is not within the scope of this book, or its author. As with charity, the first place to start is at home, by fighting for your rights and respecting the rights of those around you.

'When we talk about equal pay for equal work, women in the workplace are beginning to catch up. If we keep going at this current rate, we will achieve full equality in about 475 years. I don't know about you, but I can't wait that long.'

LYN SORANO

Now we need to back up a bit, because all of this assumes that you've already solved the dilemma of whether or not to work outside the home at all. While for some it is neither a choice nor a dilemma, for you, it may be both. Assuming you were already working when you found yourself pregnant, the first hurdle will come neatly packaged with your maternity leave – whether or not to return. Now, I'm going to break my golden rule for the second, and last, time and pass on a piece of advice, two in fact, for any mothers-to-be who may have stumbled on this book and haven't yet given up in the face of matronly cynicism, so brace yourself.

1) If you suspect in any tiny corner of your soul that you will want or need to go back to work, then make sure your job is kept open and go back. It's easier to leave if it's not working than to get it back if you decide you've made a mistake.

2) If you are going back, think you're going back or even just believe going back is in the realm of possibilities, book your childcare now, before you read another word. Quick, run to the phone and pray you haven't missed out because you weren't wise enough to book it when the line went pink (or blue). If there are no places left, feel free to curse those who were smart and dexterous enough to book during the act of conception itself.

'I KNEW I WAS GOING TO RETURN TO WORK AND UNTIL EDDIE WAS BORN, I'D JUST ASSUMED I'D PICK UP WHERE I'D LEFT OFF. AS SOON AS I HAD

HIM I KNEW I DIDN'T WANT TO WORK FULL TIME BUT I DIDN'T FEEL I WAS IN THE POSITION TO NEGOTIATE A DECENT PART-TIME PACKAGE. IN FACT, I WASN'T EVEN SURE WHAT WOULD WORK BEST FOR ME. SO I WENT BACK FULL TIME AS AGREED AND WAITED UNTIL I HAD MY FIRST SUCCESSFUL PROJECT UNDER MY BELT. THEN I NEGOTIATED A FOUR-DAY WEEK WITH THE OPTION TO WORK ONE OF THOSE DAYS FROM HOME WHEN POSSIBLE. GOING BACK AND BEING VISIBLE PUT ME IN A MUCH STRONGER POSITION. IT WAS HARD-GOING, BUT IT WAS WORTH IT IN THE LONG RUN.'

Making the decision to return to work, or not, should be, financial circumstances permitting, an entirely personal decision. Choosing to walk down a path that you have been pressured into believing is 'best' or 'right' can be a hard and lonely journey. Whether the pressure is personal or social, resistance is the only valid option. The ramifications of your decision, whichever way you go, will be far-reaching and deeply personal. You are the one who has to do the deed and the only decision that will make you happy is the one you believe is best for you. The days when women were expected to gracefully retire as part of the preparations for their wedding day are long gone. The attitude that a woman's place is in the family home still lingers.

'When I went back to work, my mother pretended to be supportive,' says Belinda, 'but she still asks, in this kind of deeply sympathetic and annoying way, "And the children, do you think they miss you?".' It drives me mad, especially because I know that intellectually, she supports my choice, but emotionally, she can't quite take it. It's easy to ignore my mother-in-law, her digs are so old-fashioned they just make me laugh. "Who will iron Geoff's shirts?" I can brush off, but my mother's question digs deep and leaves this feeling of uneasiness that wasn't there before we spoke.'

Social pressure cuts both ways when it comes to women going back to work. For every person who expects you to stay at home, there's another assuming you should be back at work. For some, choosing to stay at home can feel like a betrayal of their principles, their education and their younger self, yet going to work feels like a betrayal of their instincts as a mother. When you're caught in the gap between caring and career, the decision can be agonising.

'Staying at home never even seemed like an option,' says Mia. 'I'd worked so hard to get where I was and my job was incredibly important to me. I'd been really scathing of women who just seemed to drop off the face of the earth after they had a baby. I'd think, "How can you give up all this for that?".' Having her own baby sent Mia into a complete spin. 'I know it's a cliché, but that rush of love just blew away everything that had come before it. I did go back to work, but I just hated it. The work that had been so important to me seemed really trivial and meaningless. In my heart, I wanted to be at home but when it came to making that decision I felt paralysed. In a way I think I almost felt too embarrassed to quit.

'In the end, it was Ned who convinced me to let go of work. He just kept saying, "Do what makes you happy, Mia", until one day, it sunk in, and I quit.'

In the same way that pregnancy induces extreme myopia, it can be hard to see beyond the immediate future when you're making that first choice about work. It's not until you've travelled a fair way down the road that it becomes obvious that none of these choices has to be forever, they are really about now. What you're asking yourself is, 'Do I want to be at home while my children are babies?' not 'Am I ready to cast myself out of the world of the living for time immemorial?'.

While it's true that there are careers that cannot, or will not, survive a sustained sabbatical there is no rule that says, 'One life, one career'. That's where the flexibility comes in. In a way, mothers are the ideal modern workers. We've been told for years that the portfolio career is the way of the future and for some women a self-imposed break leads on to a new way of living and working.

'WE HIT A CRISIS POINT WHEN OLIVER WAS ABOUT 18 MONTHS OLD; MY BUSINESS WAS FLYING AND I WAS HAPPY WITH THE AMOUNT OF TIME I GOT WITH OLLIE, BUT MY MARRIAGE WAS REALLY SUFFERING. WE STARTED GOING TO COUNSELLING, AND IT TURNED OUT TO BE REALLY CATHARTIC FOR ME ON THE WORK FRONT. I WAS READY FOR A CHANGE, BUT I HADN'T BEEN ABLE TO SEE IT. I'D ACHIEVED WHAT I SET OUT TO ACHIEVE AS A DESIGNER AND NOW I WAS TAKING ON LESS CHALLENGING ROLES IN ORDER TO BE WITH OLIVER. SO MUCH OF THE PLEASURE AND CREATIVE STIMULATION THAT HAD DRIVEN ME WAS NO LONGER THERE AND SEEING THIS WAS THE IMPETUS FOR MAKING A MAJOR CAREER CHANGE. I SET A PLAN IN PLACE, RETRAINED AND SET UP ANOTHER BUSINESS, ONE THAT STIMULATED ME BUT GAVE ME MUCH GREATER CONTROL OVER MY TIME. I'VE NEVER LOOKED BACK.'

Reducing children's need for their parents' time and attention to a brief period of six months is a short-sighted game to play. It doesn't take long to discover that our memories of unbearably long days at school are perhaps a little distorted. While six hours is a long day for my kids, from my end it seems ludicrously short. School is also the time when your children start making articulate and well-planned assaults on your schedule. Sports days and assemblies are more than just dates on the calendar, they are hot spots of negotiation between demanding bosses and the job you're actually paid to do. Then there's the fundraising committee, requests to help run a stall at the fete, reading assistance, excursions, camps, and all the bells and whistles of the current curriculum. All this before you even get to the list of extra-curricular activities – soccer, tae kwon do, art, drama and tennis, and that's just the schedule of your average six-year-old. Then there's the option of after-school care and nannies, but before you know it, you can find yourself running a battery of staff and financing a frightening percentage of the GDP. 'Stepping down to spend more time with the family' may be shorthand for 'Couldn't hack it' in the business world, but it's an option a surprising number of women take.

> *'You're not obligated to win. You're obligated to keep trying to do the best you can every day.'*
>
> MARIAN WRIGHT EDELMAN

'I thought I had the whole work-life thing locked down until Jess started high school,' says Paula. 'I'd counted on it being a big transition for her but hadn't realised how much it would mean for me. The demands of her school work, activities and social life were okay, it was the huge emotional leap that came with it. We went from being really close to fighting all the time.

'One day it hit me that underneath all the shouting Jess was saying one thing, "I need you". It made me realise how much I'd relied on my mum to get through my own adolescence and I decided I wanted to be there for her and then the twins. Anyway, by then, I'd been working for 20 years and I figured I was entitled to a break.'

The quest for a proper balance between work and the rest of life will probably never fully go away, but it will diminish. I watch my mother and mother-in-law still walking the line, trading off work against time with their kids and grandkids, friends and activities, but the frantic edge that runs through my life seems to be thankfully absent. While we're in the thick of it, we can only navigate our way through it in the way that feels right and true to each of us individually and if that changes over time, or even day by day, so be it.

'Well-behaved women rarely make history.'

LAUREL THATCHER ULRICH

'BEFORE I GOT MARRIED I HAD SIX THEORIES ABOUT BRINGING UP CHILDREN; NOW I HAVE SIX CHILDREN AND NO THEORIES.'

JOHN WILMOTT

Crossing the line

*'Life is a succession of moments. To live each one is
to succeed.'*

CORITA KENT

Sometimes motherhood feels like a sprint, like when you discover you
have 20 minutes to create a non-embarrassing fairytale costume before
the school bell goes. Other times it's a marathon – staying alive through
a multi-child dose of chickenpox, anyone? Other times it's a
steeplechase, an egg-and-spoon race and a sack race all wrapped up in
one excruciating package. A life I imagined as a Sunday stroll sometimes feels like an endless race – a race against time, against mounting
bills, sagging body parts and the ever-present and uncatchable Joneses.
So when it gets too much I remember the wise words of Guillaume
Appollinaire that I filched from a horoscope one weekend, 'In the
pursuit of happiness sometimes you must stop and just be happy'.

I wish my personal race was merely about happiness, but I've taken his words to heart and whenever my mother casts an appraising eye at my mountainous washing pile, I turn to Guillame and remind myself that on my deathbed the piles of washing will have ceased to matter but the afternoons spent lying on my bed reading book after book to my babies will be the memories I treasure as I slip from this life. Well, there will be other memories, too, some that can't be printed here, others that I'm yet to experience. The point is, that hard as it all seems sometimes, chained as we are to the clock and the car, one day we'll probably be just like that old lady who smiled at you as you struggled in the playground and sighed, 'Oh, they're the best days of your life'. Better that than turning into the old lady in London who hissed at me as I struggled to get the pram through the shop door, 'People like you should stay at home!'.

The title of this chapter is a lie, it's false advertising, just like an ad for whitegoods with a beaming, glossy mother who's a scant ten years older than her fictional children. There is no line to cross, it doesn't end, it just keeps on moving ahead of us until the day we die.

I don't know that you ever stop being a mother; when I go to stay with my mother she still can't fall into a deep sleep until she's heard me stumble in and her mother still worries that my mother has too much to do. One day Mum will take Grandma's place and I'll take hers and so on down the line, assuming I'm lucky enough to have given birth to breeders, that is. We will keep spilling forth in this messy line of brand-new parents, trying and hoping, crying and laughing, and handing on the baton just as we're finally starting to get the hang of it. By then, we'll be old and invisible, and no one will want our unasked for, but hard-won, advice, which will be outdated and unusable. We'll probably be poorer than our child-free colleagues, and saggier and a little more frayed around the edges. Some of our dreams of romantic escapes and wild adventures will have been traded for another Sunday afternoon in the sandpit or on the sidelines. Our children will take us to task over the way we raised them, and then ask for help to buy a house. At one stage another of our children will have trashed our house while entrusted to sit it, ruined at least one car and driven us to the brink of a heart attack or two. There will be unsuitable boyfriends and annoying girlfriends. There will be tears, tantrums and broken tiaras (and that was just last night). There will also be afternoons in the rolling surf, rediscovering body-surfing as you pass the skill, and the thrill, down the line. There will be pride and achievement and joy. Shared memories will become a touchstone that you pass along as a precious gift for future generations. There will have been pudgy fingers to nibble on, nervous brows to soothe and spontaneous kisses to treasure. You'll always have a place on Christmas day and there will be someone to share the photo albums you laboured over. There will be the trauma of adolescence and the joys of discovering your adult children in all their real and human glory.

More than anything, when we finally get around to giving up the ghost, we'll go safe in the knowledge that we loved and were loved, that in becoming parents we weren't making a lifestyle choice, except perhaps the choice to forego one. When we had our children we were choosing to live our lives in the embrace of a family that we had the privilege of creating all by ourselves – well, maybe we had a little bit of help, but at the very, very end, there will be no one to argue over the credits with, so if you want to hog the limelight, go for your life. You deserve it.

Index

Acknowledgments

Everyone raves about their publishing team in acknowledgments, and I'm not about to buck the tradition! I've been incredibly lucky to work with such wonderful people. Diana Hill, editor extraordinaire, who was there from the conception of this book and nursed it through from infancy. Siobhán Cantrill, a truly fabulous editor, who displayed extreme patience and generosity throughout. Kay Scarlett, a great publisher with the uncanny knack of disguising from her needy authors how incredibly busy she really is! And, finally, Juliet Rogers, the kind of leader a publishing house needs – passionate, involved and extremely clever.

Personally, there are so many people to thank that if this were an awards ceremony, the band would already be playing. Old friends and new helped get me through the writing of this book. Helen Curtis has been there for ever and, thankfully, shows no signs of disappearing! Caroline Brazier: actress, artist and wonderful godmother. Tick, who has been here through all the ages and all the seas, smooth and mountainous alike. Jane Price, Sam Brampton, Jodi McLeod, Bek Perry, Kristie Phelan, Danielle Cairis, Anna Cohen, Jacquie Stepanoff, Diana Polloni, Tina Lee and the many other mothers I know and love, who helped keep me sane and entertained with the moving and hysterical stories they've shared over the years. Rachel Davis (and her mother) and Sarah Moore (and her mother and mother-in-law), who unprompted took my kids to the park, to their house, to the movies and to dinner while I panicked and wrote. Dei El-Ayoubi, Shannon Fricke and Paula Grusovin for being funny and inspiring without even trying.

And, of course, my family. My mum and dad, Brian and Vivien, for a thoroughly lovely and inspiring childhood. Patrick and Gavin, for teaching me how to stand up for myself (and marrying Vic and Fi, in turn helping create more wonderful children – Solomon, Moses, Finlay, Cameron and beautiful baby Emily). Briony, for being the best sister and aunt anyone could ask for – and not minding too much when I can't repay the favour! And, of course, for bringing Matt and Leo into all our lives. Edrei, a beautiful friend and great sister-in-law. Jonica and Liza, for helping, listening and being there! And, as I said at the beginning, Tom, Will and Sophie, my noisy, beautiful children, who have taught me so much about life, and Kiff, my gorgeous husband – together we're in with a chance of working out what the hell it all means! I love you all. Sob, sob and the band plays on.

Published by Murdoch Books Pty Limited

Murdoch Books Pty Limited Australia
Pier 8/9, 23 Hickson Road, Millers Point NSW 2000
Phone: + 61 (0) 2 8220 2000 Fax: + 61 (0) 2 8220 2558
Website: www.murdochbooks.com.au

Murdoch Books UK Limited
Erico House, 6th Floor North, 93–99 Upper Richmond Road, Putney, London SW15 2TG
Phone: + 44 (0) 20 8785 5995 Fax: + 44 (0) 20 8785 5985

Chief Executive: Juliet Rogers
Publishing Director: Kay Scarlett

Design Manager: Vivien Valk
Editor: Siobhán Cantrill
Design Concept: Toyoko Sugiwaka
Designer: Lauren Camilleri
Production: Monika Paratore

National Library of Australia Cataloguing-in-Publication Data:
Newby, Francesca.
Maternity : real stories of motherhood.
Includes index. ISBN 1 74045 742 0.
1. Motherhood. 2. Motherhood - Psychological aspects. I. Title. 306.8743

Printed in China by Midas Printing (Asia) Ltd
Text copyright © Francesca Newby 2006
Design and illustration copyright © Murdoch Books Pty Limited 2006

The names of the interviewees have been changed to protect their privacy.